THE ART OF LIVING

Well

33 Antidotes

Your Purpose. Your Journey. Your Destiny.

EROGIES GRIGLEY JR.

Library of Congress Control Number: 2021910061

Cover design by Stan Davis of MannMade Creative Consulting, LLC

Print ISBN: 978-1-09837-359-7
eBook ISBN: 978-1-09837-360-3

Printed in Pennsauken, NJ by Bookbaby.

First Edition

TABLE OF CONTENTS

THOUGHTS
FOR REASONING

Who are you?

To Whom do you belong?

Where did your spirit and soul come from?

How are you living?

What is your purpose – your truth?

Where is the destiny of your spirit and soul after death?

"Before I formed you in the womb, I knew you, before you were born, I set you apart." (Jeremiah 1:5)

"But in your great mercy you did not put an end to them or abandon them, for you are a gracious and merciful God." (Nehemiah 9:31)

"In the beginning was the Word, and the Word was with God, and the Word was God. The same was in the beginning with God. All things were made by him; and without him was not anything made that was made. In him was life; and the life was the light of men." (John 1:1-4)

ABOUT THE AUTHOR

"Because of Christ and our faith in him, we can now come boldly and confidently into God's presence." (Ephesians 3:12)

Erogies "Roe" Grigley Jr. was born before sunrise in December 1957 in Sanford, Florida to Jannie Mae Kimble Grigley and Erogies Grigley, Sr. He was born with a silvery grey patch in the center of his curly, jet-black hair. Erogies is the devoted husband to Valerie Denise Saunders Grigley, of 41 years, who he commends as his hero, best friend and lifesaver. He and Valerie are the parents of three children – Ebony, Erogies III and Erin, and five grandchildren – Amir, Aniah, Austin, Alex and Ashton. Erogies is the co-pastor of The Alabaster House Ministries, a retired Army Lieutenant Colonel and a retired federal government executive.

Erogies is committed to God's Will in helping others experience abundant living. He allows God to lead him in helping people build character, grow spiritually and intellectually, and become loving, obedient disciples. Since 1984, Erogies has found one true and faithful love that exceeds the love he has for marriage, family, humanity and for material things – and that is the love he has found in the Source, Jesus Christ. Erogies understands that each person must exercise free will choice in accepting Jesus Christ as the Source and believing in God the Father, who loves unconditionally. He believes you, the reader, will live a fuller life in the Source and Creator after reading both volumes of *The Art of Living Well*.

THANK YOU

Valerie Denise Saunders Grigley, my hero who blessed me to marry up. She has renewed me, saved my life, and has grown my mind, heart, spirit and soul to become mature in living and strong in compassion and courage.

Ebony Monique Grigley, our first child, who created family through prayer and hope.

Erogies McGee Grigley III, who pushes my character to the depths of a Dad's love.

Erin Grigley Butler, who challenges my inner strength to share my gifts from God.

Shirley Norman Taylor, JD, best friend, battle buddy for life.

Milton "Joe" Grisham, Jr., DDS, best friend, battle buddy for life.

Larry Dilligard, deacon, covenant, best friend for life.

Isaac Williams, strategist and financial genius.

Lieutenant General Leslie "Les" Smith, best friend, battle buddy for life.

Willie L. Neal, JD, minister, voice of reasoning, battle buddy from college.

Leonard L. J. Wilson, pastor, brother and friend for life.

To those who encourage me
to make others better

Amir, Aniah, Austin, Alex, Ashton - my smiles and laughter whom I rededicate to the Triune God.

Jannie Mae Grigley Harden and Lucy Terrell Bryant and my siblings who believed in me.

Erogies "Roe" Grigley, Sr. and Esther "Eddie" Cobbin McGee who loved me unconditionally.

Jesus Christ, my Lord and King. He released me to write this first book and many to come.

Special thanks to

Valerie Saunders Grigley

Erin Mone't Grigley Butler

Julian Butler

Without your honesty and candor this book would be incomplete and not fulfill the reader as designed and intended. Thank you!

THE ART OF LIVING
Well

EROGIES GRIGLEY JR.

PREFACE

The Art of Living Well begins with God the Creator and Jesus Christ the Source, and ends with you, in spirit and in truth. This book is a rarity of 33 Antidote treasures, gleamed from the 66 books of the Bible. To find success in reading *The Art of Living Well*, you must have a willingness to bend the rules of the world, but not the rules of Heaven.

The 33 Antidotes will illuminate and stir you in thought and conversation to assess your purpose, truth and your direction. The author aims to help you grasp the relationship among self, humanity and divinity that are intertwined with natural and supernatural manifestations. It is intended for this book to gently nudge you into subconscious thought and in-depth rumination. *"All Scripture is God-breathed and is useful for teaching, rebuking, correcting and training in righteousness, so that the servant of God may be thoroughly equipped for every good work." (2 Timothy 3:16-17)*

Regardless of where you are in life, where you are headed and the truthful path you should take to increase your potential for an abundant life, this book will stir a range of emotions in you. As you become enlightened by each Antidote, the desired outcome is for you to embrace your inner-person and to form a personal relationship with the Source and Creator. You will find insight into your future and accept how much the Triune God loves you and wants you to be successful. You are invaluable to the Triune God, for you are His most priceless and rarest treasure on earth.

Readers of this book are the innocent, accused, successful, heavy laden, serene, overwhelmed, wealthy, poor, as well as those looking for change, peace, direction, purpose, truth and balance. Please allow the author to acquaint and strengthen your personal relationship with Jesus Christ, so you can reach your purpose and destiny now, after death and through transitioning.

The author evaluates each Antidote by answering four questions: 1) What is the problem, issue or poison? 2) What is the antidote to remedy and combat the problem, issue or poison? 3) What are the actions to take on the path to be accountable to God and responsible to self for making a change? 4) How can you determine if you are on the path to abundant living, after remedying the problem, issue or poison?

Although there would be a societal risk in developing this book, the author prayerfully moved forth in gratitude to the Lord for choosing him to convey such a profound message to humanity. For years, the Lord guided the author's hands in humility and open-mindedness to write this book, which can defend itself against challengers, naysayers, and skeptics. *"In fact, though by this time you ought to be teachers, you need someone to teach you the elementary truths of God's word all over again. You need milk, not solid food! Anyone who lives on milk, being still an infant, is not acquainted with the teaching about righteousness. But solid food is for the mature, who by constant use have trained themselves to distinguish good from evil. Therefore, let us move beyond the elementary teachings about Christ and be taken forward to maturity, not laying again the foundation of repentance from acts that lead to death, and of faith in God for eternal life." (Hebrews 5:12-14, 6:1)*

Each Antidote opens with a quote or a Biblical scripture, providing insight to enhance the author-reader relationship, and to refine knowns and unknowns that will help you move forward in life. Refining your destiny will be met with joy, peace and harmony.

It is important to understand the format of this book:

- **Book cover** shows cherry blossoms, which represent peace and success, opposite of the unsheathed sword that represents pain and despair. The curvature highway not only separates the opposing sides, but it also signifies a rewarding journey closest to the cherry blossoms.

- **33 Antidotes** are designed to encourage meditation and conversation for days and years to come.

- **Scripture** accompanies each Antidote to provide a foundation, on wisdom and truth.

- **Special quotes** complement each Antidote to support you in facing life's challenges.

After reading this book, your new journey and direction will enable you to evict negative people and negative stress from your life. You will begin to acquire knowledge and wisdom and build a covenant of friends and expert advisors with whom you will share the existence and substance of this book. Finally, you will become part of a global conversation to promote positive change that guides humanity individually and collectively. Your willingness to be a part of something universally and spiritually special is commendable. *"I have come that they may have life, and have it to the full." (John 10:10)*

ANTIDOTE 1 |
WONDERFULLY MADE

"Once you achieve total fulfillment in learning,
you define the need for sage teachings." —Erogies Grigley Jr.

Have you ever doubted who you are or simply disliked the person you have become? Being selfish and filled with ego and pride are the false images that rob you of self-esteem and confidence. Your life should be void of low self-esteem and selfish motivations. Your life should mirror the life of Jesus Christ, in thoughts and ways, focused on how wonderfully made you are. *"Do nothing out of selfish ambition or vain conceit. Rather, in humility value others above yourselves." (Philippians 2:3)*

It is easy to let doubt creep into your life and lose focus on your aspirations. Doubt comes from a lack of trust, confidence and faith in yourself, but also in your friends, family, colleagues and Christ. When doubt is allowed to take residency, it is natural to not only lose confidence and feel like a lessor person, but also to be willing to quit. The greater the doubt, the larger the problem that appears to consume and suffocate you. During this time, life seems to cast a wide net and ensnare you in the stupidest and most painful things. You get caught up in personal, family, career and even church issues that zap your energy and self-worth. You wonder aimlessly at times, wondering 'How in the world did I allow myself to get to such a blight and dark place?' You are left to feel alone, dejected and in vain, instead of valued and loved.

Because of hurt, disappointments and deception, the tendency is for you to find fault with self and take the blame for everything that has gone wrong. Regardless of the nature of the problems, it is selfish for you to become the victim, when you are not the cause. Pride and ego can become confused with pain and hurt, causing you to refrain and acquiesce from the truth and letting the truth speak power to the person who initiated the root cause. *"But when you ask, you must believe and not doubt, because the one who doubts is like a wave of the sea, blown and tossed by the wind." (James 1:6)*

Doubting who you are leads to the decline of who you are to the point where you give into the world, thereby forsaking self and your relationship with Christ. But, wavering and being tossed amidst life challenges does not signify drowning, failure or demise. It is in this time, hesitated faith and dim outlook must be replaced with brilliance of hope, abiding faith and unshakeable belief. Understanding who you are and whose you are is knowing that you are a gift from God. You are to love (yourself tenderly,) in adoration and zeal - intimately and sensationally - beyond any regret or apology for simply being the wonderful *you.*

The Source and Creator made humankind in their likeness and image, as spirit beings wrapped in human form. Instead of focusing on selfish thoughts and desires, seek the Will of God. Present Him with the petitions of your heart. Your ever-increasing relationship with Jesus Christ will promote vision and direction. It is the Will of God to reshape and refine His people for His purpose. This shows how special you truly are.

God can mold you into being a warrior of royalty. He created you to fulfill the needs of humanity and His Kingdom. Know that you are peculiar, special and loved beyond the emotions and capacity of people, by Jesus Christ. You must fear the Lord and love the Lord, from reverence and honor, and delight in yielding to His glory. You are the Creator's joy and good pleasure, for He desires you to be holy and full of joy and happiness, through renewed attitude and faithful actions.

"Do not be conformed to this world, but be transformed by the renewing of you remind. Then, you will be able to test and approve what God's will is – his good, pleasing and perfect will." (Romans 12:2)

God choose you, His marvelous creation, to accomplish wonderful and awesome achievements in a world gone mad. Yet, in Christ, you are the shining light who can illuminate the world around you, as a light on a hill that cannot be hid. Take heart in your soul, knowing how magnificent you truly are and how important your attitude and belief in self will shape your outlook and outcomes. Think positive in the present and see yourself in an encouraging and optimistic future that beholds many wonders and favor. You can do all things your mind and hands are put to with discipline, perseverance and passion, as you walk in the center of God's Will. Embrace your connection to all people and to the beauty of the skies and heaven, which are separated by morality, mortality and eternity. In doing so, you will enjoy life beyond your limited senses where there is no remembrance of your physical body or of your cognitive inhibitions.

Together, let us cleave to all that is good in our relationship with each other and with the Lord, for this is pleasing to Him. When you honor God through obedience and delight to be in His presence, you honor yourself. Honor the Lord with all your heart, mind, spirit, body and soul, embracing an infallible truth. Have an unfailing hope that His love and esteem will always lead you to a favorable outcome, for your best interest and that exceeds your expectations.

You must have a willingness to embrace humility and kneel in obedience and reverence unto God. He sees us as we are, for who we are, and what we are (and all we do). He knew us before we were born. He loves the creation of humankind; therefore, He made us in His likeness. We are beloved by a Father who loves His children through His Son, Jesus Christ. *"We love because God first loved us." (1 John 4:19)*

Once you achieve fulfillment in learning, you will define your need for additional teachings. The greater the fulfillment, the more you will enjoy the works of the Spirit and mind of the Source and Creator. You will find that your purpose is not limited to vocation, rather to your passion and convictions. Your purpose encompasses higher perspectives that promise to increase your faith.

Of course, you are being led by the Creator's Spirit, and you will develop a lifestyle that encompasses work, prayer, fellowship and the study of God's Word. This includes the reading of complimentary books to increase knowledge, wisdom and understanding, which are necessary for the betterment of your heart, mind, spirit, body and soul. To be in the center of His Will, you must trust God. You must be made pure by allowing God's thoughts and ways to lead yours – which are as far from God as the east is from the west and the north is from the south. Thus, you cannot rely on self to know all things. You must be led by the Source and Creator. Savor the faithfulness of God to know what is best for you, for He will guide your thoughts and direct your ways in all things earthly and Heavenly. *"Trust in the Lord with all your heart and lean not to your own understanding; In all your ways submit to Him and He shall make your paths straight. Do not be wise in your own eyes." (Proverbs 3:5-7)*

It is the person of the Holy Spirit who desires to align your thoughts, attitudes and habits to His will. Your ways and your personality will become pleasing as you take on the character and gifts of the Holy Spirit. God honors the righteous and just, the beloved friend and the obedient disciple who strives to live in the Spirit. So, persevere in faith. Keep the commandments. Love Him and care for His people. These tenants are guaranteed to please God and promise unspeakable joy, unsurpassed peace and unimaginable serenity – all yielding an intimate relationship with God.

God offers a reservoir of grace and mercy to those who chase after His heart. As you keep His commandments, you will recognize that you are righteous even though you were born in sin. You must choose to be hot or cold. God will not make the choice for you. Preferably, you will choose to be hot, embracing servitude as a passion for Christ and service to people – along with other divinely led disciples, past, present and future. *"Do your best to present yourself to God as one approved, a worker who does not need to be ashamed and who correctly handles the word of truth." (2 Timothy 2:15)*

Comparably to the past, people may see these as negative features and might become distrainable and confused. Remember, everyone does not do all things in love for others or in support of those less fortunate. Only through living in truth are you able to edify humanity and glorify the Divinity seated on the Mercy Seat. God desires to give you the imperishable gifts of grace and mercy with a promise of eternal life.

You will transform towards heavenly enlightenment by discovering your identity and giving rumination to the grand design of Heaven and earth. You will come into divine understanding when your roles in both purpose and assignment are achieved. As you move through repentance, forgiveness and obedience Christ will continue to enlighten you for the glory of the Father. Only then can God transform the more perfect person inside of you. To have His thoughts and to be filled with the beauty of a personal relationship will enable you to mature in His principles and statues. As this spiritual wisdom evolves, you will matriculate greatness through Christ, upon which you should ruminate day and night.

God's desire is for you to reach a spiritual level that affords you the freedom to make ethical decisions and personal choices. Once filled with the Holy Spirit of Jesus Christ, every breath and every moment can be taken with boldness to reach high standards and to achieve successful outcomes. Consider measuring your life by the day, instead of by the years. In other words, measure each day in what you have done to improve yourself and by how you have helped someone in need. Each day, you should evaluate how you have helped to change another person's life for the better. Ask yourself how you have taken a stand for a cause worth living or dying for. You will realize that with God's help, you have accomplished more than your expectations. *"I pray that out of his glorious riches he may strengthen you with power through his Spirit in your inner being, so that Christ may dwell in your hearts through faith. And I pray that you, being rooted and established in love, may have power, together with all the Lord's holy people, to grasp how wide and long and high and deep is the love of Christ, and to know this love that surpasses knowledge." (Ephesians 3: 16-18)*

No one can reach the maturity level of the unconditional love that Jesus Christ offers. Nor can He be taken away once you have invited Him into your heart. You are His church, who has all of His love as that of a bride. God promised to abolish the number one threat to His Church. This threat is under the spiritual rule of Lucifer, who is commonly known as Satan. Lucifer rules the world through un-renewed minds and through religious people of unbelief. In contrast, Heaven has nothing that fades, degrades or diminishes. In Heaven, there are no crimes or sirens. No grieving mothers or fathers. No rebellious children. No orphanages. No wars or discriminations. No divorces. No immoral theatrics. Stress, disappointments, the need for mirrors to appease vanity or a moment of confusion between dislike and distrust will not occur in Heaven. Finally, the grief and emptiness of death comes to an end, and eternal life is found. *"I will give you a new heart and put a new spirit in you; I will remove from you your heart of stone and give you a heart of flesh. And I will put my Spirit in you and move you to follow my decrees and be careful to keep my laws." (Ezekiel 36: 26-27)*

In the near future, the Lord will reign and be pleased with His re-creation of the Garden in the New Zion. It is God's Will that as it is in Heaven, be it the same on earth. Those who love Him and keep His commandments will do great deeds and will love and forgive all. The beloved and faithful shall live in the great City of Zion where Jesus Christ reigns. These tenants of Bountiful Instructions Beheld Living on Earth (B.I.B.L.E.) will completely strengthen you. God provides an infilling with essential foundations for your journey along the right path. He will guide and bless every step taken towards your destiny.

As you can see, God has made you wonderfully for His purpose. All else is self-fulfillment, self-promotion, delusion and vanity. In the likeness and image of the Source and Creator, you must hold to your position as being a disciple and a ministering friend. First, you must minister to yourself, family, your circle of friends and to your neighbor. Teach the Word and share enlightenment for abundant living. This mature journey can take a lifetime, but for some, the inner divinity and truth is manifested early.

Your enlightenment will begin as a wonderful life that is filled with purpose. Embrace the enlightenment and spiritual change in you. Take a leap of faith into your vision. Only then can you influence the path of others – regardless of their living conditions. God will be well pleased with your obedience. *"Because God wanted to make the unchanging nature of his purpose very clear to the heirs of what was promised, he confirmed it with an oath. God did this so that, by two unchangeable things in which it is impossible for God to lie, we who have fled to take hold of the hope set before us may be greatly encouraged. We have this hope as an anchor for the soul, firm and secure." (Hebrews 6: 17-19)*

The path of Enlightenment (God's divine Word) for your Journey (harmonious spiritual living) will be made clear for your Purpose (God's Will) and will spiritually lead you during your Destinations (assignments) towards your Destiny (returning your soul and spirit to God). Your arrival in Paradise (eternal life), not Hades (eternal damnation), will allow you to enter the doorway of your Heavenly Home (New Zion).

The art of living well is summed up through your demonstrated faith, honored works of giving, and obedience in perseverance. Helping others move towards abundant living will increase their personal relationship with Jesus Christ – all while recalibrating the inner-person and building great faith and trust in Him. Continuously seek the Kingdom. Daily execute your progressive works for God's Will and keep great faith in all endeavors. Never be lukewarm, but instead respond to the clarion callings from Jesus Christ.

It is my sincere prayer that the Master's work of this antidote has already begun to enhance your spiritual curiosity. And, as the sweet fragrance rises from the pages, may the words take your mind, heart and spirit to flight for greater enlightenment and for abundant living. For you were created in the image and likeness of the Source and Creator. You were fearfully and wonderfully made.

> *"As a prisoner for the Lord, then, I urge you to live a life worthy*
> *for the calling you have received. Be completely humble and gentle;*
> *be patient, bearing one another in love. Make every*
> *effort to keep the unity of the Spirit through the bond of peace."*
> *(Ephesians 4:1-3)*

ANTIDOTE 2 |
LIVING BEGINS WITH
THE SOURCE

"Each day, be reminded that you are made just a little lower
than the angels, but a magnificent, cherished, beloved
and adopted child in the family of the Most High God."
—Erogies Grigley Jr.

Are your beliefs grounded in prideful, egotistical and worldly desires? Are you facing these vipers that keep your heart from being pliable and filled with joy and happiness from the love of another and the Father? When your heart's attitude collides with a foul mind, you become cold and callous towards people and life, and never fulfill very much. There is a fine line between the ethos of love and the learnt behavior of hate and pride, which is void of relationships and being on one accord. *"He became stiff-necked and hardened his heart and would not turn to the LORD." (2 Chronicles 36:13)*

You cannot fully live until you defy the heart and the mind. A harden heart and apprehensive mindset creates pain, hurt, distrust, loss and betrayal. The viper's bite is poisonous, causing swelling, infection, delusion and separation; and if left untreated, even death. Toxins of worldly living are quick. Many times, the strike is not seen until the bite happens. It is critically important to focus on the love of God and the love for self. Without God's love, you will not be able withstand the venom of the viper.

The good news is that there is a striking connection between the heart and the mind. "As a man thinketh, so is he in his heart." The decision to give your life to Christ takes the sting and poison out of the venomous bite that wants to suck the life out of living abundantly. The bite is quick and painful. The poisons of anger, pride, ego, hurt and low self-esteem moves rapidly, and the impending damage can be devastating if help is not obtained immediately. The heart and mind *must* be guarded at all costs, doing what you can to slow the toxin from getting into your bloodstream. So too is sin, which threatens to bring hurt, harm and lost to you. Living a sinful life is dangerous to not have a personal relationship with Jesus. Without the right diagnosis and anti-venom, death is imminent. Without Jesus Christ, abundant living is fleeting, and eternal death is certain.

The response to this threat is just as swift and potent. The treatment for the deadly poison that enters the bloodstream *must* respond to the anti-toxins. No sooner than the mouth utters words that connects the heart with the mind - making the decision to follow Jesus is imminently made - and help is immediate. When your relationship is not personal with the Lord, you cannot expect for Him to respond to your 911 prayer call. Many fail to realize that God's Spirit is the power within that can overcome the viper's bite. God desires and seeks for all to have a relationship with Him and to live a wonderful and bountiful life. But He will not violate your free will to choose life or death. Many snakebites are preventable and certainly treatable to prevent death, recover and live a long quality life. The bite of a venomous viper does not translate into death. If you are grounded in the Lord, your heart is not hardened to the world, then you do not need to panic.

First, you must be aware that there is a problem, either sensing or seeing the viper person in your life. The problems can range from unbelief, worldly desires, materialism, ego, pride and immoral thoughts and undesired behavior. Usually, vipers appear within people in your life and places where you spend time. Let go of people, places and things that are detrimental to a relationship with the Lord

The knowledge and understanding from this expository and prose are rare and highly effective antidotes for you to possess and embrace, to prevent and treat venomous and non-venomous spiritual, mental and emotional bites. God's highest aim is to help you grasp the relationship between humanity and divinity, the human spirit and the Spirit of the Lord. In order to experience the natural and supernatural manifestations of antidotes, God must gently heal your heart and lead you into subconscious thought. Such as ruminating and marveling about the Creator and the Source - His thoughts and ways as a part of your life. Understanding how much the Source loves you, is the rarest of treasures to possess.

The Source made humankind in His likeness and image, as spirit beings, which creates His awesomeness to reshape and refine His people for His purpose. God can lead you to become a caretaker, warrior, entrepreneur, steward or anything to fulfill the needs of humanity. Remember, success in *The Art of Living Well* must find you willing to bend the rules of the world and keep His Word hidden in your heart and written on your mind. You must seek the will of God and present Him with the petitions of your heart's desires.

"Take delight in the LORD, and he will give you the desires of your heart. Commit your way to the LORD; trust in him and he will do this: He will make your righteous reward shine like the dawn, your vindication like the noonday sun." (Psalm 37: 4-6)

Your belief, confession and ever-growing relationship with Jesus Christ promotes living in harmony with a vision and direction for purpose. Your faith will increase in the Creator and His faithfulness towards you. If you reach a place of prideful totality of learning, you will find no need for additional teachings. Such a prideful attitude will limit biblical and spiritual applications of living. The greater the fulfillment, the greater you will enjoy the work of hands and mind, in spirit and in truth. This experience plays a vital part in the release of your purpose and truth (destiny), to increase your faith in the Source and Creator, as well as in self. Certainly, no one can compare, and no one can ever reach the maturity level of the unconditional love offered by Christ. You must embrace your connection to people and to nature in order to grow in your walk with the Source. Watch the beauty of the skies which expand to the universe and the cosmos, separating life by time and space to heaven, rather than by distance. There is neither time nor space because each moment of Heavenly life is enjoyed beyond the fullness of your limited emotions. There is no comparison or remembrance of our physical bodies and cognitive brain inhibitions once we are with Jesus Christ.

God abolishes the number one discriminator of His people (church) that earth embraces as a religion. In Heaven, there is nothing that fades, degrades or diminishes; no sirens at night, no criminals or crime. No crying mothers over a kidnapped child. No empty-hearted fathers of a wayward son. No funerals. No wars. No discrimination and hatred. No personal drama. No homelessness, poor, hungered or downtrodden. No abusive relationships. No dead-beat dads. No movies or evasive reality shows of fake housewives and unruly men. No trashy music. No videos of ignorance, crime, feuding, murders, facades and lies. No illusions. No self-projected pride to be number one. No greed and selfish desires for accumulating money to live a lifestyle displeasing to the Creator. No stress. No appointments to be late to. No concern or need for mirrors to look at your vanity, and not one moment of confusion or emotions embedding dislike or distrust. And finally, death is defeated, forever! *"Death has been swallowed up in victory. Where, O Death, is your victory? Where, O death, is your sting?" (1 Corinthians 15:54-55)*

You are being led by the Creator's Spirit as you develop a comfortable lifestyle and good way of life. In this Spirit-led life, your life will be encompassed with good work, prayer, fellowship, the study of God's Word and complimentary books to gain knowledge, wisdom and understanding. These are breathed from the knowledge each day to better you in heart, mind, body, spirit and soul and to face and defeat the assured challenges and tribulations that are always near the path of *the art of living*. You will transform your spirit towards enlightenment upon giving thought to the grand design of Heaven and earth. As a disciple, you must contemplate your role in life with purpose and assignments where Christ will surely usher enlightenment to you. The Source will reshape and form the more perfect person inside of you, according to His ways and thoughts. To do so, He must have your heart, mind, spirit, body and soul. These thoughts are filled with the beauty of progressive growth in principles and virtues, which you can demonstrate honorably and nobly. As you ruminate on the Scriptures, Christ's influence will guide you to reach your best ethical decisions and personal choices. Once done, every moment taken in small and great strides can be measured daily to determine successes and outcomes. Allow the Source to guide you towards pleasing habits, strong work-ethics, and sound character towards reaching your fulfillment. *"Jesus asked them: 'Why are you talking about having no bread? Do you still not see or understand? Are your hearts hardened?'" (Mark 8:17)*

God honors the righteous and obedient, the friend and the disciple who strives to live in Spirit, discipline, truth and love. He honors the one who perseveres in faith on the journey, in loving Him, caring for people and managing the earth. You must not travel someone else's path, for this is not the Will of the Lord, nor is it your truth. These tenants are guaranteed to please God and promise unspeakable joy, unsurpassed peace and unimaginable grace with an intimate relationship with Jesus Christ and God the Father.

God offered better promises of His salvation, unlimited grace and mercy through Christ for the committed who chase after His heart on earth. Those who fully keep God's commandments know fully well that they are righteous, though born into sin. In this path, it is best to resist learning and courting the ways of the world. It is best to refrain from being lukewarm so that the finishing of the inner self can be sincere in humility to Christ. Within life and with God, family and friends, you must choose to be hot. You cannot keep your hands from the work and expect success, harvest or God's favor. The Source will not make the choice for you. You must make a mature decision that is founded in wisdom and character. Being hot or cold is the willingness and courage to take a position or not take a position towards purpose and cause in Christ, speaking power to truths and truths to power. You should be girded in righteousness, riding on faith and producing good works. You must stand for something, or you will stand for nothing and no one. The Source gives you a free will spirit to choose and to act, not to be idle and full of fear. He gave you a heart, mind, spirit and soul to be victorious and brave. Any life lived where you are less than hot or cold, less than forthright and courageous, is not a life worth living. *"I know your deeds, that you are neither cold nor hot. I wish you were either one or the other! So, because you are lukewarm – neither hot nor cold – I am about to spit you out of my mouth." (Revelation 3:15-16)*

Each new day, as it is in Heaven, God desires that we live a life in His promises for love, joy, peace and harmony. If you love Him and keep His commandments and keep the faith, you will do great deeds and will love and forgive all. You shall see the Great Day and experience majestic moments. You shall live in the new city of Zion where Jesus Christ reigns as the true King of Kings. These tenants will be the essential foundations critical to an abundant and eternal life. The tenants are necessary for your journey on the right path and will guide every step towards your destiny, which is returning to Paradise with the Source and Creator. *"And I heard a loud voice from the throne saying, 'Look! God's dwelling place is now among the people, and he will dwell with them. They will be his people, and God himself will be with them and be their God. He will wipe away every tear from their eyes. There will be no more death.'" (Revelation 21:3)*

Having a positive and committed attitude and with good works unto the Lord will help you grow by recalibrating your free will each day. You will also experience callings from Christ and to do the Will of God. When you perceive spiritual revelations that heaven, earth and all therein are creations of God the Father, you will find balance in life. You will be bound to Jesus Christ by His light and easy yoke. During this era (transition), it is common to think this type of living would become too challenging and confusing; however, the just and strong will stand and share His good news story. Christ lives, and He desires to give you the gifts of salvation, grace, mercy and an abundant life. *"We have different gifts, according to the grace given to each of us."* (Romans 12:6)

The Creator places each person on earth for His purpose, which is to understand their divine purpose. All else is self-fulfillment, self-promotion, delusional and vanity. As the likeness and image of Christ, you must embrace the position in life of serving and ministering. You are a servant of God and a minister of Christ. First to your family, circle of friends and neighbor, then to humanity. You should exhibit consistent demonstrations of love and compassion, grace and mercy to those you care for. As a servant minister, you are responsible for sharing and teaching the Word to those willing to hear for enlightenment and understanding of Christ's life applications. Reaching this maturity in your journey can take a lifetime, as you continue to grow to please the Lord and to help make someone's life better. But for some, the inner divinity is manifested early, and the change to enlightenment begins. Embrace enlightenment and spiritual change in you and for you, with a humble and pure heart. Only then can you stretch your mind to influence someone's principles, thinking, actions, liberties and path, regardless of the environment. In this enlightenment phase, the divine Creator, God Almighty, will find you well-pleased through His beloved son Jesus Christ.

The path of enlightenment in God's divine word for your journey of spiritual living will be made clear. He will lead you to your destiny (returning your soul and spirit to God) for your eternal status (paradise to eternal life). *The art of living well* is reached through your demonstrated acts and meaningful works towards others, which pleases the Lord. It is my belief that the words of this book have begun to give flight to your mind for a change in perspective towards the greater you. God created you in His image, likened to the Son, who created all creations that inherited a more excellent name above all names.

"Jesus answered, 'I am the way and the truth and the life.
No one comes to the Father except through me.
If you really know me, you will know my Father as well.
From now on, you do know him and have seen him." (John 14:6-7)

ANTIDOTE 3 |
JUSTIFIED WITH THE SOURCE

"Great and joyous is the day to enter awareness and full knowledge of being made one with Jesus Christ, as in being a part of the Spirit of God through Christ." Erogies Grigley Jr.

Do you feel pain and hurt from being born into a difficult life? Although you were created in the likeness and image of the Source and Creator, because of the transgression in the Garden, you were born into a complex and challenging world. In the carnal mind of humankind, you were filled with a sinful nature and were prone to the influences of evil spirits – spirits that desire to inhabit the minds and thoughts of people by creating trials, tribulations and sorrow. *"The Lord is close to the brokenhearted and saves those who are crushed in spirit." (Psalm 34:18)*

So many people have only known pain, hardship, fighting, poverty, injustice and suffering their entire lives, which causes life-long bruises and scars. This life is attributed to no fault of their own. Rather, they were born unequal and in a lesser status than someone born in a land of milk and honey, along with freedoms and liberties. This unfortunate news may come as a disagreement, but if you compare their lives to others, especially those born in fourth and fifth world undeveloped war-torn countries, you would conclude you live under grace and mercy.

Many people live under the Biblical laws and the laws of government, yet the laws fail in protecting and providing. Some people use laws to justify their actions and lifestyles. Others hide behind the laws for power over those of lesser status. Confirming to laws are good but embracing the law without living a spirit-filled life above the law, limits a personal relationship with Jesus Christ and those of honor and virtues. There can be no joyous and measured successful life under the law, if you are consumed with living under and being justified by the law. For a joyous life in Christ, you must surrender to Him as your Savior, for deeds will not replace salvation by grace. *"You who are trying to be justified by the law have been alienated from Christ; you have fallen away from grace. For through the Spirit we eagerly await by faith the righteousness for which we hope."* (Galatians 5:4-5)

Today, there are hundreds of different types of manmade gods that people worship and rest all their hopes in. These gods are made in the minds of people and are without immortal facts and history. We worship people and things without realizing such a person or thing has become an idol in our lives. Such as a home, car, money, job, child or even your mate. Yes, as we mature in our personal relationship with Christ, we should be thankful for our blessings of family and favor.

There is redemption, hope and a bright future if you reverence Jesus Christ as Lord and Savior. To trust and have abiding faith in God is wise and prevents you from being a part of foolishness and falling away from His grace, mercy and joy. For we do not seek the things we can see visibly, but those things which we hope for as evidence and assurance of our faith in Christ. (Hebrews 11:1)

You need His faithfulness and grace. His grace is the unmerited, unearned favor of God based on truth and trusting faith. Although we did nothing and can do nothing to earn God's grace, we can receive His grace through faithfulness and love. Without these two working together, everything that happens is meaningless and of little to no value. For the evidence is in the facts that are built on nothing less than an abiding faith, working by love, for which you were justified through grace. You see, without an abiding faith in God's faithfulness, it is impossible for you to dine in His favor and enjoy His table of rewards. And, you cannot please Him without faith.

It is imperative that you stand firmly on the foundation of the Biblical tenants of Jesus Christ; not only for self, but also for family, friends and survival of humanity. Without a committed and submissive heart, mankind have less of a promise for a successful and long life. *"Beyond all question, the mystery from which true godliness springs is great: He appeared in the flesh, was vindicated by the Spirit, was seen by angels, was preached among the nations, was believed on in the world, was taken up in glory." (1 Timothy 3:16)*

People and technology have contributed to the advancement of life; however, advantages and disadvantages have evolved from inventions and advances. Although life is better for some, everyone does not fully enjoy the bounties from tremendous and successful advancements. You cannot put your trust in these, for you limit your possibilities in the grace of God. But, fret not and do not lose heart or hope, for God is able to do exceedingly abundant in your life. Because of the glorious sacrifice of Jesus Christ, the Source, we are one with God and have power and dominion over all principalities of darkness and evil in this world. We are in the world, but not of the world. Thereby, we cannot be fooled by the fallen one, Lucifer. We are adopted heirs to the Kingdom of Heaven and will share in God's glory now and forever. *"Therefore, since we have been justified through faith, we have peace with God through our Lord Jesus Christ." (Romans 5:1)*

God was asked who He should say He was when people asked who sent His representative, and what name should be given? God responded to His representative: *"'Tell them 'I Am Who I Am' have sent you!'" (Exodus 3:14)* When examining the eight words, glimpse the depth of who God is in Christ and who Christ is to you. He is saying, I am all that there is,

I am all that was and will be, and I am all that you need. God is saying, I don't change, I am the same yesterday, today and tomorrow and I am the Sovereign and Omnipotent Creator who cannot lie and cannot die. You are precious in the sight of God and you are joyous to Him, which is why He chose you.

Many things are spiritual; therefore, you have the power to change what happens in your life. It is through grace that you have control of your life and can influence your family and friends. Invite Jesus Christ as Lord to operate in your heart and spirit. You are in charge of your soul, and you must make the decision to give your soul to Christ. He will not violate your decision. Everyone who accepts Christ as Lord and Savior is His beloved child, many of whom He is well pleased and extends His unconditional love that is founded on an old covenant agreement by God with His people. When you believe in the Triune God, a new Covenant is established, and you accept Jesus Christ as Mediator and Intercessor to go before God on your behalf. Your faith and good works move Jesus Christ the Lord and God as you chase after His heart! *"Now devote your heart and soul to seeking the LORD your God." (1 Chronicles 22:19)*

Scripture records that in the beginning there was a presence of someone with God during creation. You can reach the conclusion that this someone was His one and only loving Son, Jesus Christ. For scripture records: *"In the beginning was the word, the word was with God, and the word was God." (John 1:1)* The Word is none other than our majestic Savior, Jesus Christ. Therefore, you are given opportunity to be forgiven and redeemed in this life. As such, you should give honor, glory and praise to Jesus Christ as Intercessor unto God. He has no beginning and no ending, and all things, including heaven, earth and the universe were created by Him. He also holds all things of creation together, for all came from God, through Christ, and Christ is the only way to God. Jesus, the creative and compassionate Christ, was there from the beginning with greater compassion and love than that of His Father's wrath.

Each day be reminded that you are made just a little lower than the angels but magnificently cherished as a son and daughter in the family of the Most High God. You are God's leadership choice to cultivate and manage the earth while studying the cosmos and its succinct order. As a member of this present age, and of ancestors who belonged to the likeness and image of the Creator and the Source, you are today's family inheritors. You are the constant to *the art of living well* and should prepare life for future family members who will continue the legacy. You are born with a calling upon your life – a calling into the institution of God's Kingdom family and earth's humanity. In your given purpose, you recognize the yearning towards the predestined and free will choices as you travel and traverse along a path – called a journey of life. Life happens more abundantly and vividly when you make a committed decision to live in the inspired, redeemed or reclaimed moment, regardless of your situation. Let go of circumstances!

The advancement of technology has skyrocketed throughout time. Years ago, it took days to travel from one state to another. People only had access to a land line phone and three television channels in the home. Today, it only takes a few hours to get from one state to another or to conduct transatlantic and transpacific travels to other countries by air. Internet and cellular service have created real time access to almost anything and anyone – allowing us to perform face-time interactions where we no longer just hear one another by voice. With the conveniences of advanced technologies, it is rare for families to have dinner together at the family table. Missing out on sharing intriguing stories, songs, and the Good News of the Gospel that prepare us for life, both earthly and eternal.

Because of a lesser desire for conversations, no longer is it commonplace to write letters to a parent or friend. Rather, texting and using social media are preferred choices to convey life's activities. These systems are beyond great. But with these phenomenal times comes the great loss of sound and longstanding values that should be instilled in children or discussed by adults to ensure proper guidelines for decision making and wise interpretations of emotions and experiences.

In this new age, many adults have given way for their children to become victims of worldly views of life. And, unhealthy introductions through television, Internet, social media, music and videos for children's six-inch square minds have become the battlefield of despair. The enemy has mis-used advanced technologies to target a strategic territory and to lure us towards lifestyles of illicit behaviors and possible acts of evilness. Life is far from the simple life of yesteryear's challenges of being home before dark. Today is filled with unheralded challenges of everything accessible on a computer, iPhone and television that trick even the noblest of persons.

Why did Jesus Christ go to the cross and stay on the cross? He could have called 62,000 warrior angels, but He did not. He went willingly to the cross because He reverenced His Father, and He stayed on the cross because He loves you. Only through His death could He make Heaven and earth right through restoration and redemption. Only through His death could He make right the first and last transgressions made by man. He persevered through His sufferings and death in order to return and take His rightful place in Heaven with God the Father. His perfect sacrifice for the atonement of all sin settled the act of disobedience by man, so sin is no longer punishable through death without a chance for salvation and eternal life. Jesus Christ paid every debt in full – once and for all – with His divine and perfect human life. His crucifixion redeemed you, and His resurrection took away the sting of death and replaced it with salvation and eternal life.

Not only that, but His ascension to Heaven enabled Him to include your name in the Lamb's Book of Life, which only Jesus Christ has the authority and power to open. He Himself writes the names of His beloved children in the Book of Life! Never forget this truth of Jesus Christ, for He is coming again, and He will judge you in due season, for every account of your earthly life, both good works and unpleasing works. The shared attitude and knowledge also go to the enlightened with wisdom and understanding. Know and be fully persuaded that you also are the "I am" in Jesus Christ, and Jesus Christ is the "I Am" in God. You are made righteous and justified by Christ's faithfulness and your faith, to be able to appear before God. Grace has been given to each of us as Christ apportioned it. This is why the Bible says: *"He who descended is the very one who ascended higher than all the heavens, in order to fill the whole universe." (Ephesians 4:10)*

You, who belong to Jesus Christ, should be full of faith and obedience, striving to keep the Scriptures. Those who are peculiarly and wonderfully made, and keep the faith are important to God. It was a great day to enter awareness of being made one with Jesus Christ, as in being a part of the Spirit of God through Christ.

Your life is filled with free will choices, some with fewer freedoms and liberties, but all choices and decisions are accompanied with a purpose. You are placed from birth on the path of *the art of living well*. Your first crawl to your first initiated action has been a journey towards your destiny. Strive to stay on the true path, even though there will be knowns, unknowns and detours as a result of your free will choices. You must ensure your course of navigation, for delays and accelerated gaits of difficulties on the path will impact the journey's offerings. Opportunities, which might come with a price, will require sacrifice in the physical realm and in the spiritual cosmos.

The greatest price has been paid, for the Source did so as the only acceptable ransom. The perfect chosen Lamb and only begotten Son of

God, sent by God the Creator for your faults and imperfections, lessened your price. Remain committed in faithfulness to Him and His commandments. *"Just as the Son of Man did not come to be served, but to serve, and to give his life as a ransom for many." (Matthew 20:28)*

Once maturing in mind, body, spirit and soul in both the Word and in a relationship with the Lord, you are ready to begin the journey along the abundant path of life. The personal price and life's cost are required in advance and during the journey. Before the personal price is satisfied, the cost comes into existence, which is that of a Spirit-led change to be or not to be Christlike. This price is in the form of your faith, your character, your values and your obedience. The cost is to give up the former life, which was not pleasing to the Lord, and embrace the new life, which is being in the center of God's Will and keeping His commandments. *"I want to know Christ – yes, to know the power of his resurrection and participation in his sufferings, becoming like him in his death." (Philippians 3:10)*

You must embrace the richness of your lineage and heritage, not simply as a person, a human, or member of society. You are a part of the family of royalty and richness, marvelous and wonderfully made, created in the likeness and image of majesty. You are esteemed by the Source and Creator of life with full privileges as a beloved birthright heir. The perspectives are where you have acquired a made-up mind in principles and in attitude of spirit. Reach for the level of spiritual maturity and put childish and worldly ways behind you. Let the mature person rise, the wise and honorable person, who is full of the Spirit and who is obedient to the Scriptures. Rise up and embrace *the art of living well* in Jesus Christ! *The art of living well* is in the "I am", knowing that you are not your own and you cannot control things within your own power. Command all things through the Source and the Creator who said, *"I AM, WHO I AM"*, is my name when asked! (Exodus 3:14)

"Until we all reach unity in the faith and in the knowledge of the Son of God and become mature, attaining to the whole measure of the fullness of Christ. Then we will no longer be infants, tossed back and forth by the waves, and blown here and there by every wind of teaching and by the cunning and craftiness of people in their deceitful scheming. Instead, speaking the truth in love, we will grow to become in every respect the mature body of him who is the head, that is, Christ." (Ephesians 4:13-15)

ANTIDOTE 4 |
ALWAYS MAKE THE CREATOR
AND SOURCE FIRST

"He is the beginning and end, as your intercessor and true love."
Erogies Grigley Jr.

Who do you and people say that you are? Do you believe living abundantly refers to understanding who the "I Am" is in your life? Until you know who you are and to whom you belong, you can never discover your true purpose or travel your journey with abundant living. To know who you are is to find the answers to what you believe, what you stand for, and where you want to be in the future. To find the answers to these questions, you must first experience true love. *"It always protects, always trust, always hope, always perseveres." (1 Corinthian 13:7)*

All should give honor, glory and majesty to Jesus Christ, for He has no beginning and no end. All things include heaven and earth, and the universes were created by Him and He holds all things together. Jesus was there from the beginning as the Source. He loves you and only through His death could He with the Father settle sin and death once and for all; redeeming you and taking away the sting of death!

Never forget the truth that Jesus Christ is coming again! The shared attitude and knowledge go to the enlightened, so you should know and be fully persuaded that He is the "I Am" in Jesus Christ, and Jesus Christ is the "I Am" in God. *"We have much to say about this, but it is hard to make it clear to you because you no longer try to understand. In fact, though by this time you ought to be teachers, you need someone to teach you the elementary truths of God's word all over again. You need milk, not solid food. Anyone who lives on milk , being still an infant, is not acquainted with the teaching about righteousness. But solid food is for the mature, who by constant use have trained themselves to distinguish good from evil." (Hebrews 5:11-14)*

A person who belongs shares in the richness and royalty of being peculiarly and wonderfully made of spirit, soul, heart and body, with a mind as the unique, but far less cognitively in-depth as Christ. It was a great day to enter into the full knowledge that we are made just a little lower than the angels. We are magnificent and cherished as a child, son, daughter and adopted believer in the family of the Most High. You are in the present age, from yesterday's living of your ancestors who belonged in the likeness and image of the Creator and Source, and tomorrow's family inheritors who are the very constant to *the art of living well.* You were born with a purpose and calling into the institution of God's family and humanity referred to as life. A Christlike life happens in living in the moment of your environment with discipline, wisdom, understanding and embracing God's way of life, in the midst of free will choices, some with less freedoms and liberties.

You should strive to stay on the path and avoid detours on the journey in time and space, as the path is filled with dangers, seen and unseen. The greatest price has been paid and the cost endured, for the Source did so as the only acceptable ransom, as the perfect and only begotten Son of God. This gift of love lessens your personal tribulations and prices paid for making bad choices. Dependent on your spiritual and conscious decisions, you journey along the path of life either towards successes or towards failures. The payment was required in advance before the journey began. You must resist the desire for worldly satisfactions that seduce and destroy you. The world shares no shame, in anything that tares you into pieces and breaks your heart!

You must feel, know, see and say "I am" in Christ and made a little lower than the angels. *The art of living well* is in the divine blossoms of love in spirit and truth, while getting wisdom and understanding. These character traits are Heavenly, spiritual and divine in the glorious spiritual nature of God. You must become fully and indelibly cemented in your importance to God and the Source, for their Will as one, for your life and purpose. Highly value your life as the first fruit of God with a promise and covenant to be of significance in the earth's operation and evolution. The surrender and acceptance that you are a child of God comes with perks, benefits and privileges beyond your greatest or miraculous expectations.

Feel, know, see and say "I am" near to the Holy One as a friend, who was made above the angels and given all power, authority and dominion in Heaven and on earth. As you reverence the Master, the Savior, fully embrace the free gift of adoption into His spiritual family and the inheritances of God, the Creator and in Jesus Christ, the Source. If you do not value and respect yourself, as only you know self, much less than God knows you, you are no good to self or to your circle of life. Most people error by their ignorance of the power of God that is within their realm, and the lack of power externally in the world not under their control.

Do you always feel the need to be in control or to be the team leader in a sport or in life? Does it have to be about your will? Do you know that the Will of God is there all the time? His Will prevents bad things from happening to you, as you are covered in His grace? Do you know that God is a jealous God, and His Will is perfect for your life, now and in eternity? It is God's Will and law that you never be indebted to man or corporations. In the same way, Christ did not take the glory of becoming a king. Instead, God said to Him, *"You are my Son; today I have become your Father."* *(Hebrews 5:5)*

31

Because you make sacrifices to live a pleasing life unto the Lord, there is always the presence of the Source's glory on your obedience and life. This relationship of Father and child, also as Master to friend is founded in the Agape love of a spiritual and favored relationship with God and Jesus Christ, with the Holy Spirit as one. However, most people rarely share their testimonies of testing, failure, suffering, trials and tattered shoes walked in. You can go to the Source at all times, to commune with the Lord in a personal and intimate relationship. It is in this relationship that resides a personal covenant founded on better promises and unconditional love. In these tenants and covenant agreements, you find an abundance of blessings and favor, even amid the greatest challenges, tests, trials, storms and losses. *"The LORD will open the heavens, the storehouse of his bounty, to send rain on your land in season and to bless all the work of your hands. You will lend to many nations but will borrow from none. The Lord will make you the head, not the tail." (Deuteronomy 28:12-13)*

Regardless of where you are in life and how life looks, your present position, state and location is not your final destination. It is a place that you got yourself to, God allowed Satan to put you there, or God Himself put you in a situation to get your attention. It is awesome that God can take you higher and refine your transformation from being less than average to above average, to the esteem of going from bad to good, good to great, in adoring and uplifting Him, first. Your daily way of life, words and earnest lifestyle should be toward the Lord, himself. He will make your enemies your footstools, for the battle is His, the victory is yours, and the Lord gets all the glory.

The art of living well becomes a reality when you surrender to the higher calling and understanding that you are under a higher authority. You did not evolve from an animal or apes. Rather, the Source and the Creator created you and you are HIS special creation. You have been made specifically in God's likeness and image, as beings, with a spirit and a soul received from the Lord. This wisdom and understanding are paramount to walking in the light and living a life abundantly in the divine blossoms of love, spirit, giving, and serving, while growing and gaining friendships in the Kingdom of God. Many people live to eat, instead of eating to live. The same is likened to some people who live to be in the world with a life of excitement and risk, instead of only being of the world to live a life pleasing to the Lord and finding favor throughout life. Everyone must have a regard for the authority to whom one is responsible and accountable – Jesus Christ.

To live honorably, just and disciplined, morally and spiritually, are the Heavenly character traits that causes the Source and Creator to smile on your life, which bring smiles and laughter to their hearts. You must place significant value to your life, which is drawn to the Source's bosom, wrapped in His loving arms and under His wings of protection. For in this pure heir and friend relationship rests great promises and a grand covenant. When you surrender to God and His Son, your heart, mind, body, spirit and soul surrenders. This path leads all fleshly desires to correction and submission as an accepted child of God, with grace, mercy, restoration and spiritual privileges, manifested in the physical actions and blessings of your life.

This relationship is exquisitely beautiful and one of great meaning and purpose. For you will feel, know, see and say "I am" one with the Holy One and the Lord, who Himself is above the angels and all manner of beings. The Creator has given the Source all power, authority and dominion in Heaven and on earth, over the world and the evil one. Understanding the "I am" in the "I Am that I Am" fully embraces the joyous and magnificent gift of adoption as children and heirs into the spiritual family of God, the Creator and in Jesus Christ, the Source. You must value, respect and treasure your significant importance to the Source, and acknowledge it is to Him, whom you belong. In this conviction, not only will you become good to yourself, but also to family, friends and the Kingdom of God.

Never allow yourself to become a victim of twisted truths and false pretense, under the guise of fellow co-heirs, based on greed, ignorance, pride, selfishness and vain conceit. Rather, know assuredly with abiding belief in your heart, the power within and the power to call upon, in the time of need and rescue. *"Yours, LORD, is the greatness and the power and the glory and the majesty and the splendor, for everything in heaven and earth is yours." (1 Chronicles 29:11)*

Because you are a part of the family of royalty and richness in Christ, in unconditional love and excellence of support with the Lord, the perspective should be that you are one with a made-up mind to live for the Source. Are you satisfied and full of joy to know what it means to live the journey in purpose for Christ, because of what He willingly did and continues to do for you? *"The Son is the radiance of God's glory and the exact representation of his being, sustaining all things by his powerful word. After he had provided purification for sins, he sat down at the right hand of the Majesty in heaven." (Hebrews 1:3)*

Jesus was divinity and an unveiling of God's Spirit in the flesh. His birth and living are the greatest of life, for His birth meant the coming of salvation and His resurrection means forgiveness and life instead of death for all who will believe. And out of His humility, servitude and greatness, comes the favor and blessings of God, His Father; where both were deeply satisfied in His works which prepared a pathway to victorious living. Nothing or no other can make Him love you less than what he desires and purposes! But first, you must believe in Christ and love Christ regardless of the cost. Never be indebted to any man, but, with all of your heart, mind, spirit, body and soul, be indebted and obedient to Christ!

"For to which of the angels did God ever say, "You are my Son;
today I have become your Father"? Or again,
"I will be his Father, and he will be my Son?" (Hebrews 1:5)

ANTIDOTE 5 |
A HIGHER AUTHORITY

"Thoughtfulness in the beginning, through rumination and reflection leads to a peaceful, balanced and joyous long life." Erogies Grigley Jr.

Who are you responsible and accountable to as a higher authority? Are you constantly fretting and doubting who you are and fretting over the decisions that you have made in life? Do you judge and question why other people seem to be better than you? There comes a time in life when you must look in the mirror and see your reflection staring into your eyes with truth. You are who you believe you can become, with the help, hope, faith and trust of the Source who does greater works in you. *"And we all, who with unveiled faces contemplate the Lord's glory, are being transformed into his image with ever-increasing glory, which comes from the Lord, who is the Spirit." (2 Corinthians 3:18)*

In the beginning was a cosmic explosion, beyond time and space, beyond the heavens, beyond existence. Within this explosion was power, purpose and provisions for a new creation by the Source and Creator. The explosion was the roaring and mighty voice of the Lord. As God's Spirit moved over His creation there was emptiness and no form of life. There was a short period of darkness during the void of life, as the Source and Creator spoke aloud. This darkness, which contains no existence, disappeared under the voice of the Source and Creator. *"God said, 'Let there be*

light!' God saw that the light was good. So he divided the light from the dark-
ness. God named the light 'day' and the darkness 'night'." (Genesis 1:3-5)

As the Creator and the Source, His Word spoke all into existence, and morning was separated from evening, all things were created, divided, separated and made with oneness in connection and dependency of the other by the Source. But, when the air was divided from the water, dry landed developed, the seas were gathered, and plantation produced, and the Creator and Source found this to be good in their sight. But it was the creation of mankind that won the Creator's heart, mind, spirit and soul. After the creation of the first man, made in His likeness and image, God blew His Spirit into the man and breathed the breath of life. Then, the Creator placed man in the special Garden and gave him dominion authority over everything in it, alone with the wonderful helper woman, who He created for man. *"And God said, 'Let us make man in our image, after our likeness: and let them have dominion...' So God created man in his own image, in the image of God created he him; male and female created he them. And God blessed them..." (Genesis 1:26-28)*

You must embrace the high idea of being accountable to a higher authority, rather than to self and man. This high idea is shaped in the knowledge and understanding of accepting humility of self in the eyes of the greatest of all, Jesus Christ. Living to serve the Source and Creator in simple obedience and abiding faith, for they are Sovereign and true, in all ways and all days.

Have you discovered who the Source and Creator is to you? There is great evidence that you are from the Source and existed in spirit before taking on a tabernacle of flesh. You were not just born one day or night on earth. You were not simply created by the union of mother and father. Your life is from the Source as a spirit with God before being formed in your mother's womb, as a fertilized egg from the man's fertilization. Before you were born, you shared a relationship in spirit with the Source and Creator in Heaven. For God said He knew you before, expressing to whom you belong and to who you are from. *"Before I formed you in the womb, I knew you, before you were born, I set you apart." (Jeremiah 1:5)*

Why is the Triune God – Father, Son and Holy Spirit – so vital in your life? Do you fully trust the Lord? *"In the past, God spoke to our ancestors through the prophets…, but in the last days he has spoken to us by his Son, whom he appointed heir of all things, and through whom also he made the universe. The Son is the radiance of God's glory and the exact representation of his being, sustaining all things by his powerful word. So he became as much superior to the angels as the name he has inherited is superior to theirs." (Hebrews 1:1-4)*

Your supernatural power is in transcending the old, to become enlightened by the Holy Spirit to begin living in God's grace and mercy. Having a renewed mind and reshaped heart for a noticeable change, which illuminates your knowledge, wisdom, and understanding in the relationship and the spiritual anointing with the Lord. Now, feel and embrace the change in your: Perspectives, Principles, Path, Thinking, Actions and Liberties – for your journey along the path to your destiny! Every good gift comes from God, -- you must believe this and begin your life's journey! You are not the source of what you receive – it all belongs to and was made available to you as a steward by God. *"David praised the LORD in the presence of the whole assembly, saying, "Praise be to you LORD… Yours, LORD, is the greatness and power and the glory and the majesty and the splendor, for everything in heaven and earth is yours. Yours, LORD, is the kingdom; you are exalted as head over all. In your hands are strength and power to exalt and give strength to all." (1 Chronicles 29:10-12)*

Stay on the path of righteousness in life. Take no detour or exit road. In the broadest of day and lurking of darkness lay trouble from spiritual wolves, vipers, locusts, leeches, grasshoppers and scoffers to trick your mind, so they can steal, kill and destroy you. But there is good news if you stay in the center of God's Will near the cherry blossoms. Jesus is on the

37

throne, and He has appointed angels with assignment to watch over and keep you from dangers seen and unseen. His glorious Will cannot take you where His Sovereign grace and authority will not provide protection, provisions and purpose with power for you.

Trust in the Lord and hear His voice, as He also shows you divine signs to move in His Will and purpose which He places on your life. Live in your overflow of grace, mercy and faithfulness to keep you, to give you peace and joy and to call you His own before men and before God. He cancels all of your debts, so you can be a cheerful and bountiful giver unto God, the church, widows, orphans, the sick and the poor – those transformed to be near God! When the high idea of who you are intercedes with where you are in your personal relationship with the Holy Spirit, then you will know fully that the Source and Creator knew you from your beginning and will know you in your never ending!

"Consider it pure joy, my brothers and sisters,
whenever you face trials of many kinds, because you know
that the testing of your faith produces perseverance. Let perseverance finish its
work so that you may be mature and complete,
not lacking anything. If any of you lacks wisdom, you should ask God, who
gives generously to all with finding fault,
and it will be given to you. But when you ask, you must believe
and not doubt, because the one who doubts is like a wave of the sea, being tossed
by the wind. That person should not expect to receive
anything from the Lord. Such a person is double-minded
and unstable in all they do." (James 1:1-8)

ANTIDOTE 6 |
LET CHRIST RESIDE IN YOUR LIFE

"One who extends humility within self to give,
will embrace this same compassion." Erogies Grigley Jr.

Are you finding it difficult to fulfill the mission of Christ in sharing the truth and good news of the Gospel of God's Word and His life? You may find it uncomfortable and a daunting task, as you grow from being a babe in ministry to a mature believer in Christ. The more you exercise your faith, the easier it is to fulfill His mission. How do you see yourself in Christ? Accept the love of God and you will be changed for the better and known for living an abundant life. *"For now we see only a reflection as in a mirror; then we shall see face to face. Now I know in part; then I shall know fully, even as I am fully known." (1 Corinthians 13:12)*

The aim is to ensure people around the world discover Jesus Christ and enter into a personal loving relationship with Him and God the Father, for living an abundant filled life! Regardless of your draw or lot in life, despite your timing, overlooking your place in life, you are important in the eyes of Christ. Therefore, let enlightenment and understanding grace you, for Christ to equip you as a new or seasoned believer. To be inspired in biblical stories to become more knowledgeable of the spirit-filled life through Christ as the Source. The Creator offers a relevant and practical way to communicate the truth through wisdom, knowledge and understanding, to produce enlightenment and restoration. This results in strengthening you, regardless of age, into a mature, wiser, committed, better, stronger and spiritually producing disciple of Christ. You become grounded in the unified family and community in the body of Christ, on one accord.

God promised to make Abraham a nation of many. He looked around, and there was no one else greater than him to swear by. So, God swore, "*I will surely bless you and make your descendants as numerous as the stars in the sky and as the sand on the seashore.*" *(Genesis 22:17)* Making your descendants numerous upon the earth for Kingdom building is pleasing to God.

It should be your heart's desire to have the Lord's promises of blessings on your life, based on your belief, faithfulness, obedience, good works, and love. Abraham was obedient and full of faith, and in God's due season, just as Abraham received what God promised him, you also will receive what God has promised you through Christ Jesus. The scriptures say that "*People swear by someone greater than themselves… This is the way and thoughts of the Lord and God, which we all should live accordingly.*" *(Hebrews 6:13-16)*

There is a passionate appeal that your understanding matures with the presence of the Source Jesus Christ and God the Creator, who are Omnipotent and Sovereign to forgive and bless you along your journey to *the art of living well.* You can expect to learn from Christ as the Mediator and Master while serving others and not judging others. He is the only one truly capable of judging your life for the future kingdom, as He reigns as king and is faithful to those that know and love him.

If you humble yourself to receive the Lord Jesus Christ as your personal Savior and reverence God as your Creator, you will extend God's compassion to your family and to everyone you meet. At all times, share the Good News of the Gospel of Christ, for the purpose of salvation and a great hope for the future to those that will hear. Trust that in the presence of God and Jesus Christ, you can have hope. There is faithfulness in a loving God and Son of God who will give you power, vision of destiny, clear instructions and great patience to be careful and bold in Christ. As you travel the path of life, be cautious of detours to the left and the right. Be confident that God will guide you towards your destiny, which is paradise and Heaven. *"In the presence of God and of Christ Jesus, who will judge the living and the dead, and in view of his appearing and his kingdom, I give you this charge: Preach the word; be prepared in season and out of season; correct, rebuke and encourage--with great patience and careful instruction." (2 Timothy 4:1-2)*

When a person is a true disciple of God, the repentant new believer receives God and the Son of God as their personal savior and Lord of their life. He is your ransom – having paid the price in exchange for the freedom of your life, instead of you receiving the pain and punishment He suffered instead. He wants you to be free and fully healed, belonging to him in the future. Jesus Christ, the Savior and Messiah, made this decision for you long before the foundation of the earth, universe and cosmos were formed. In these difficult days, learn to trust and rest in God. He has already promised to prosper you and to not let harm come to you and your home.

Because of your committed belief in Christ's virgin birth, He is divinity wrapped in humanity as the one and only begotten Son of God that paid the only acceptable ransom to God His Father. He ensures that you can be redeemed, and that you can place all your faith and hope in Christ, as He is the only way to God the Father. As a strong disciple that chases after Christ's heart with God, the glory of Christ is available to you. As God's children, He places love in your heart for all people, yet while hating the sinful behavior of all people. *"For I know the thoughts that I think toward you, saith the LORD, thoughts of peace, and not of evil, to give you an expected end." (Jeremiah 29:11)*

It pleased God that His Son Jesus Christ was willing to suffer and die as a human being – all to temper God's wrath and punishment to the remnants of the earth. However, it is superlative in the shed blood of Christ that moved God for the account in which Christ did such an awesome, magnanimous and glorious act. The act that serves as the only acceptable and worthy consideration and ransom for humankind's account of ceasing to live corruptible lives. Because of Christ's shed blood, the only barrier between forgiveness and God granting clemency is sin and one's unwillingness to repent. Without Christ's sacrifice, it would be impossible to achieve His principles of righteousness, truth and justice. When Christ is removed, the effect of peace and a long life would be completely different and justice to sinners would have to be carried out as God's wrath. Repentance and salvation, through the shedding of the precious blood Christ, simply and greatly enabled one to be pardoned of all sins, to be forgiven and share in entering into Heaven. Yet, the new life of a believer will learn of Christ's cross to prove a life that is of God in Christ on earth. You must live each day for eternal life, when the day comes for you to die. And in death, you will rise and forever reign with Christ, for you are filled with the living water of Christ and living Word of God. (Ephesians 4:1, Hebrews 13:15, 1 Peter 2:5, 1 Peter 1:19-22)

There is nothing or no one greater on the earth and throughout the universe than our Lord and God. For He swore to Himself, by Himself, to bless and care for the people He made who live in His likeness and image. *"When God made his promise to Abraham, since there was no one greater for him to swear by, by himself, saying, 'I will surely bless you and give you many descendants.' And so after waiting patiently, Abraham received what was promised." (Hebrews 6:13-15)*

There is no greater pursuit than to seek after Jesus Christ and God the Father. Invite Him into your life and heart. Make Him your Lord and Savior. Sup with Him and confess that you believe He was crucified, died, and that God His Father raised Him from the dead. It is the desire of Jesus that you become a student and bearer of the Scriptures of the Good News Gospel for yourself and carry it to all people. Christ established this principle and commandment when He said, *"I give you this charge: Preach the word; be prepared in season and out of season; correct, rebuke and encourage – with great patience and careful instruction." (2 Timothy 4:1-2)*

The careful words of a commandment aligned with the Scriptures is for you to study to show you are approved before God and men. In order to be a wise, courageous and firm disciple of faith, you must be filled with the indwelling of the Holy Spirit; learn how to resist the enemy and overcome the stumbling blocks of sin called challengers and deceivers. *"Study to shew thyself approved unto God, a workman that needeth not to be ashamed, rightly dividing the word of truth." (2 Timothy 2:15)*

You cannot continue to live and expect growth if you rely only on your family's traditions and rituals, which may depart away from the Scriptures, as well as pastors and elders who take the law of God to shackle you to cult-like, principles and practices. You must be holy in everything you do, just as God who chose you is holy. The Scriptures say, *"You must be holy because I am holy. And remember that the heavenly Father to whom you pray has no favorites. He will judge or reward you according to what you do. And the ransom he paid was not mere gold or silver. It was the precious blood of Christ, the sinless, spotless Lamb of God." (1 Peter 1:15-19)*

You must learn from personal study of God's Word and grow in a daily relationship with Jesus Christ of what is truth, power, the way, and the life of the Lord. Even today, many people talk Christianity but live and teach religious fascism with false arguments and misrepresentations of Scripture that lead babes in Christ down wrong pathways. Some never tasting meat, not knowing the benefits beyond that of milk. Once you grow into a dynamic disciple, developed from dynamic teachings and per-sonal study, while living God's Word, you come into the wisdom of the factual existence that the precious blood of Jesus Christ is filled with love and hope. Christ is "All" as the only begotten Son of God who thought not selfishly but volunteered to give us His glory with the Father, which existed long before there was a world. *"And to make it your ambition to lead a quiet life: You should mind your own business and work with your hands, just as we told you." (1 Thessalonians 4:11)*

Christ, who was unblemished, volunteered to become the sin offering. His blood cleanses all who repents, as He is the only acceptable atonement for the sins of the world. His blood will be acceptable until Christ returns to earth as King. Christ's noble sacrifice produced the efficacy of grace and gave the Holy Spirit to every believer, for mercy and comfort. Regardless of race, gender, ethnicity or background, you bear a right to Christ's new covenant, unlike ever before, founded on better promises. (Hebrews 1:2, 1 John 3:8)

"See what great love the Father has lavished on us,
that we should be called children of God! And that is what we are!
The reason the world does not know us is that it did not know him. Dear
friends, now we are children of God, and what we will be has not yet been
made known. But we know that when Christ appears,
we shall be like him, for we shall see him as he is." (1 John 3: 1-2)

ANTIDOTE 7 |
THE PRICE WAS PAID

"Whether life is filled with moments of abasing and abounding, sufficient is the grace and love of Jesus Christ." Erogies Grigley Jr.

Have you been robbed of your joy and happiness? Rejection and unbelief can lead to a state of guilt, helplessness and despair, which begets depression and isolation. You must find the strength to persevere. You do not know what the future holds, but you do know that you are in the Will of the One who holds the future in His hands. *"Encourage your hearts and strengthen you in every good deed and word." (2 Thessalonians 2:17)*

You will either find personal favor or rejection of doors and windows of life that open and close. But, in the Source, you can experience both binding burdens and loosening exceeding joys. Jesus Christ is the Master and Mediator, being sufficient in our abasing and abounding. For in the Source and Creator, you can do all things that are the Will of the Lord. Before grace came faith, where all were guarded under the Law of governance and obedience to God's instruction. *"Know that a person is not justified by the works of the Law, but by faith in Jesus Christ. So we, too, have put our faith in Christ Jesus that we may be justified by faith in Christ and not by the works of the law, because by the works of the law no one will be justified." (Galatians 2:16)* The law remains as instructions for obedience, discipline and guidance until Jesus Christ will make one righteous through salvation, justified by faith, having been sanctified and glorified by His crucifixion, death, burial, resurrection, ascension and coming again.

We are all God's children through spirit and faith in Jesus Christ the Source and His unwavering faithfulness and unconditional love. We who believe and are baptized into Christ have willingly and lovingly been clothed with Christ as His children and ambassadors. There is no separation of Christ's children, not through race or ethnicity. We are all brothers and sisters through Adam and Abraham, Eve and Sarah, and we are made one family in Christ Jesus as His descendants. We are the righteous adopted heirs to the blessings of an inheritance with better promises and a new covenant in Jesus Christ, with God the Father.

What was the price?

The price was for Jesus Christ to leave His deity in Heaven to sit at the right hand of God on the throne of creation, life and existence; and to suffer horrifically and experience death, for the resurrection by God the Father. He experienced the fullness of life as a human being on earth as a fetus, infant, boy and man in which he was clothed a little lower than the angels in flesh and wrapped in His divine being. The price was for Jesus Christ to be tormented, whipped, beaten, spit on, stripped naked and nailed with spikes to an old rugged wooden cross for all to witness. They laughed and wagered bets that He was listed as King of the Jews. He foreknew that the price included His Father allowing Him to be tormented. The price required Him to be crucified and His blood to be shed for the remission of all sin, disease, sickness, pain, hurt, hunger, poverty, all matter of evilness and even death. *"This is my blood of the covenant, which is poured out for many for the forgiveness of sins." (Matthews 26:28)*

It was for the manifestation of truth to come forth that the Romans and Jews murdered not only the King of the Jews but the Lord of Lords and Savior of the world. Jesus willingly paid the price by giving His life, which He had the power to deny or the access to ask His Father God to call the whole matter off. The price for humanity is for you to deny self and demonstrate humility, love, obedience, discipline and forgiveness as a lifestyle. You must have a willingness to die to sin for Christ and live in His ways as a way of life, unto God the Father, for their glory, as your good pleasure.

The ransom of His deity and life was required to hide all believers' sins from God the Father and Creator, and to cleanse every person's heart that accepted Him as Savior and Lord. How long would He last before dying, as well as, endure the consistent teasing and shouts from the rebel crowd of Jews, Romans and others to save Himself if He was the Son of God. But, with all of the glorious power residing in Him, the divine ability to command millions of warring angels available to Him, and the choice to call on God to stop the madness and evil, He did not give up, because of you. He remained humble in deity and took on the venomous verbal assaults of the accusers and spectators. He endured the horrific pains, debilitating emotions of delusions, hurtful ignorance, and physical and mental anguish of men and women who lived in the world under enslavement. He was overwhelmed by being crucified because religious leaders who feared His great following. *"But how is it to your credit if you receive a beating for doing wrong and endure it? But if you suffer for doing good and you endure it, this is commendable before God. To this you were called, because Christ suffered for you, leaving you an example, that you should follow in his steps. 'He committed no sin, and no deceit was found in his mouth.'"* (1 Peter 2:20-22)

Jesus Christ had to be true and noble to respect Himself, faithful to the promise He made to God the Father, and committed to become a child in the flesh, having been born in a manger for a home. He bore all sins. He took on all sickness and every imperfection, emotion of anger, bitterness and despair. He replaced hate and vengeance with forgiveness and love. He took hopelessness and replaced it with salvation and took on the sting of death, replacing it with eternal life.

The manifestation of truth did come forth, where the Romans and Jews conspired together as Pharisees, and Sadducees, along with the mob of citizens who murdered the Lord of Lords. Jesus willingly paid the price and suffered the cost by freely giving His life and laying down His spirit, which He had the power to overcome. The price for humanity is for you to deny self, accept Jesus Christ as Savior and choose to live in submission to His Will. The cost for humanity is to adhere to Christ's commands for one's actions to demonstrate belief, love, obedience and forgiveness as a lifestyle, while keeping the faith and trusting in the Source.

In order to become Christlike on earth as it is in Heaven, your life must be an example of Christ's life. You must mature in heart, mind, spirit and soul in your relationship with Christ so that self is least important in His purpose. Embrace a willingness if necessary, to give all you have to the poor, to die for Christ so that others might live in His ways and His Will by your example. Submit yourself unto the Source, our Lord and God the Father, for the Trinity's glory, as being your good pleasure. Show gratefulness for being recognized by Christ, as His well done and beloved good servant.

What was the cost?

The cost was for Jesus Christ to freely accept being separated from His Father through death for three days, going into hell and facing Satan and all of his demonic angels. Yet, He conquered death and bruised Satan through God's power and resurrection of His spirit and body. He faced and defeated the evil fallen angels that knew Him personally before they were cast out of Heaven. After the sting of death was removed, the keys to the gates of hell were returned to the owner's possession, into Christ's bruised, yet strong protective hands.

Now, after God raised Him from the dead, and He ascended to Heaven to take His rightful seat on the throne next to the right hand of God. Jesus could now lead all believers in Him unto salvation and eternal life as His children, dead and alive. Now, because of His embraced cost, your cost is to deny self, pride and vanity, sacrifice absence from the worldly sinful ways and thoughts, and receive Christ's open invitation. You can accept the Source as Lord and Savior of your life with a new heart and renewed mind. The Creator, as God the Father, of the Lord Jesus Christ, will accept your repentance of sins. Ask the Source for forgiveness, as Lord of your life. Pray! Turn from worldly ways, and, seek the face and heart of the Lord! *"If anyone comes to me and does not hate father and mother, wife and children, brothers and sisters – yes, even their own life – such a person cannot be my disciple. And whoever does not carry their cross and follow me cannot be my disciple."* (Luke 14:26-27)

We know that God loves Jesus in the highest of agape love as His one and only begotten Son. So much, because He was like His Father and He laid down His life, trusting His Father to raise Him up for the salvation of humanity to have a second chance and to be redeemed. Not only that, but Jesus's life was too powerful for someone to take. No one could take His life, neither could He give His life before or after the appointed time for Him to lay it down of His own accord. He was the only one with the authority to lay His life down in death. And, by His Father's authority, Jesus Christ was raised up again, receiving all authority and power in Heaven and on earth from God the Father.

Today, you must lay down your life freely from sin and the world, and Christ will give you the power to raise it in repentance and forgiveness. Jesus Christ paid the price and suffered the cost for Him to be able to transform you in this life and transcend you in death to Paradise. He will raise you up again from death, too eternal life with Him, God, the angels and hosts of Heaven. You must love others, for the Lord to cover you in His grace and fill your heart with compassion for humankind, sometimes above your needs and priorities.

Lucifer and the angels knew Jesus personally and Jesus's separation in death would be without warring angels and ministering angels. Jesus promised to embrace the cost to replace burnt unblemished animal sacrifices and replace them with His perfect and sinless body of deity and humanity and unblemished shed blood to purge all people who believed in the Creator and the Source. Then, He healed the land and homes of those who believed. Jesus was buried in a borrowed tomb and entered into hell to take on Satan and all of his fallen angels alone and defeat them. During this supernatural simultaneous spiritual and human being experience, He significantly injured Satan and humbled death to take its sting away from humanity. He ensured salvation to believers and ensured once again that the Lamb's Book of Life was secure. As Jesus was crucified, God and all of Heaven waited for His blood to hit the Mercy Seat where He had sat next to His Father. God resurrected His Son in three days and gave Him all power and authority in Heaven and on earth. Again, after the sting of death was removed, the keys to the gates of Hell returned to the owner's possession, Jesus Christ, King of Kings, Lord of Lords.

Now Christ was ready, having taught the gospel and established His church upon a solid rock, His Word, to leave His Redeemed Gentiles and Jews with the Holy Spirit and a new covenant. This was a covenant founded on better promises to ascend to Heaven to sit again on the throne at the right hand of God and serve as Mediator and Intercessor. Jesus could now lead all believers in Him in faith unto salvation, grace, mercy and eternal life as His children, dead and alive. Now, it is imperative to see this state of grace, mercy and love, because of His commitment, obedience and perseverance to drink from the bitter cup. The cup that would lead to death and separation from His Father was magnanimous and a priceless cost for redemption and restoration of those He loved first. *"Do not take revenge, my dear friends, but leave room for God's wrath, for it is written: 'It is mine to avenge; I will repay," says the Lord." (Romans 12:19)*

50

Therefore, you must refrain from trying to get even with others. Christ died so He would take on your offenders and abusers, and you would be able to let the wrath of God settle any debt against you. Do not worry about what a person thinks of you and tries to do you harm, for God will judge for the just, those called by His name, against all persecutors, He will repay. If you are not a part of the problem or solution, you are a gossiper and the problem to a problem. You must resist from becoming a part of an indifference and disagreement between others, unless you are the solution. When you reason over an issue, you will normally find there is not a problem; rather, you are the problem that created the phantom. Remove yourself from the environment and climate so that the conditions change. When there is a concern with someone, have a conversation with the person and you may discover there isn't a problem; you just need to talk to clear any misunderstandings and ignorance. Living is in communicating and trying your best to live peaceably, as much as your character allows, with all people. *"If it be possible, as much as lieth in you, live peaceably with all men." (Romans 12:18)*

In Christ's sacrifice, your cost is to deny self, resist avenging, sacrifice absence from the world and worldly sinful ways and thoughts. Receive Jesus Christ's invitation extended to your mind, heart and spirit, so you can freely accept the Source as Lord and Savior of your life with a renewed mind, spirit and cleansed heart. In this moment of acceptance and making Christ your Lord and Savior, the Creator as God the Father, of the Source, there also is the acceptance of repentance for sins. This act allows the Source to forgive and save all who opens the door of their lives and hearts to the One who knocks, as Lord of their lives. Humble yourself, pray, turn from worldly ways, seek the face and heart of the Lord in order for the price He paid, the cost He had to endure and deity He had to give up to save you. He is sufficient to return you to Him as His own. Love others equally in agape love, for the Lord to cover you in His grace, tender new mercies and fill your heart with compassion for humankind. Often times, this requires placing the Will of God above your needs and priorities, for the Lord to love you unconditionally and faithfully. Doing so, you will increase in humility and grow in your relationship with Christ and His power operating inside of you through the Holy Spirit.

Why was the price so high and the cost so great?

The price came as a ransom paid in full and the cost as a perfect sacrificial offering substitution by the Source, atoning you from sin for the remainder of your earthly and eternal days. In addition, now you can be with Christ in Paradise and live with Him after death spiritually in His new city, called Zion, where you will know the full measure of being a part of His royal court. The price and the cost required committed suffering, sacrifice, humbled surrender, dying and burying old self, to rise from baptism as a new person and to keep the Word of God burnt in your mind and buried in your heart. Through His Spirit and ascension into Heaven sitting at the right hand of God allows the infilling of the Holy Spirit to all who turn from sin and embrace Christ as Lord and Savior. He will help all who come to Him as disciples, giving each person joy, peace, abundant living and unconditional love for the remainder of your days in *the art of living well*. Being righteous and holy upon the earth and above the Law should be the aim of every believer. These glorious benefits and perks heavily outweigh and broadly cover the wages of sin, through the end of this age. *"For there is one God and one mediator between God and mankind, the man Christ Jesus..." (1 Timothy 2:5-6)*

Beloved, I would have you to know, you are not alone. God will never place more on you than you can bear with His help and grace. Nor will His perfect Will take you where His grace and love will not provide provisions, promises and protection to accompany you. When you are saved and sanctified as a believer of Christ's family, you will always be attached to God, who

God Himself said in the Scriptures, to tell anyone who asks who sent you, *"My name is "I Am Who I Am" and say 'I Am has sent me to you.'"* *(Exodus 3:14)*

There is no greater aspect of living than a life filled with peaceful mornings and nights, living spiritually and righteously, and striving to be holy as the Source and the Creator. This attitude and lifestyle are glorious and pleasing for the personal and intimate spiritual connection and growing relationship with Jesus Christ, whose name is "Wonderful", "Counselor", "Mighty", as our Source, Mediator and Intercessor. His Will is simple for your will, ways and thoughts to succumb to Him as your superior Lord and Father. Convert to His Will, thoughts and ways, for your purpose on earth, in spirit and truth, manifesting through faith, obedience and good works in physical and spiritual deeds, with glorious results pleasing unto the Lord. There is none and nothing more important and precious to the Lord than you! He desires to delight in your growing relationship with Him through the Holy Spirit, who is your wonderful guide, helper, counselor and petitioner unto Christ and before God on the throne of righteousness and Christ seated on the Mercy Seat.

Out of darkness, God the Creator and Jesus Christ the Source created the universe, cosmos and humankind and breathed the breath of life into man for His joy and companionship. Then, the Creator rested, for He was pleased with His creation, the soul wrapped in His divine nature, into which He blew His divine spirit into the creation to give man life. This new creation with woman was marvelous and a complex flesh of persons, shaped in the Lord's likeness and image, as great joy was spawned into living vessels and agents for God's purpose and glory. As you reach a mature age to form your right personal decisions and good choices focused on pleasing the Lord, you will realize that you have the available resources to cover the price, and you also have the capacity and surplus to give to others toward enduring the cost. Deny self and place the Lord as your master. Love Him and your neighbor, fellow men, women and children. If you choose to, you will be able to travel farther along the path of life during your journey and relationship with the Source, covered in His grace, led by His love and glory, and followed by goodness and mercy, all of your days.

The abundance of life's treasures is in the Triune God and spiritual relationship of covenant fellowship with the one He called His own, and with whom He is well pleased! The Source first loved you, which is why we love. It is a great deal that Jesus first loved you and loved you so much that He was willing to do anything in His Father's Will for you! Is this not the greatest love and reasoning sufficient for you to love and live with joy? *"We love because He first loved us." (1 John 4:19)*

God took a portion of His divine nature, upon which He laid your soul, wrapping the two into one. His divine power is the connection to everything you need for a holy character and spiritually abundant life, for your purpose on earth and in Heaven for God's Will. The chosen one who shares a spiritual relationship with the Source is one with both He and God. You will receive the fertile knowledge, sage wisdom and spiritual miraculous powers of the glorious One, the Son Jesus Christ. He is the only One able to give grace, mercy, holiness and Fruit of the Spirit as delightful fruit for each day. He alone bears Gifts of the Spirit to your prayers, supernatural acts of miracles in answering the prayers of others and giving hope for anyone. By your belief, connection and daily communion in prayer and conversations with the Source, you are able to resist conforming to the patterns of the world. Resist the darkness that lurks in the corners of the earth, with the sole intent to smoother humanity with evilness, and to enslave you to sin that binds humanity and the earth from its liberties and freedoms.

The Source loosens your shackles from sin, lights your home brightly so that darkness can flee and speaks a word to cause evil to tremble and dash away into the abyss in great fear. His love, power and authority enable you to make the most of your time, in each season of your journey, along the path of living to be transformed and refined in the renewing of your mind. Along the path, foolishness, ignorance and sin are to be avoided at every temptation along your journey. Temptations are plentiful from the cast down, unworthy, unloved angel Lucifer, alias name Satan. His temptations are only through you allowing his thoughts in your carnal mind when it is not under subjection to the Holy Spirit. The Source marvels and enjoys showing He is no respecter of person, not even on His favored ones, who are able to test and prove God's Will and blessings for your purpose in *the art of living well.* This is the critical link of supping with Christ consistently and daily, along the path in your journey. For Christ's love is agape, very good, expressively pleasing, unconditionally perfect and without end.

The Source and Creator knew all, and all to come in your life, before you were formed in your mother's womb. You came from the Creator as a spiritual being, with an uncontaminated soul, a flawless character, through time and space to inhabit the earth for a purpose. In this enlightenment, you must transcend mere logic and rationale of mankind. Embrace your identity and path of living spiritually with a pre-determined desired destiny to guarantee the spirit and soul a personal relationship with the Source and Creator. Your personal choice to believe and accept Jesus Christ as Lord and Savior, is the only way to solidify and bind the covenant agreement. The covenant with your belief, guarantees returning your soul and spirit to Heaven and enjoying eternal life with the Son of God and God the Father, after death. *"My frame was not hidden from You, When I was made in secret, and skillfully wrought in the depths of the earth." (Psalm 139:15)*

You understand the Source's Will for your existence and purpose, out of the Creator's divine Will and inseparableness, He pours forth His anointing to strengthen you when you get weak in your flesh and weary in spirit. God constantly surrounds His beloved friends with ministering angels and equips them with spiritual gifting powers. He has the spiritual powers to accompany your great faith to be secure in His Will, covered in His divine grace and supplied with provisions to be ministered to and protected by selected and appointed angels. You can be assured that in His divine and dominion authority and power of His Will, you can go forth in your assignment with boldness, courage and peace. You can have the full knowledge that God's Will shall be accomplished through you and that God will not forsake you, no matter the test or trial.

In all matters of existence in life, you must have a set of guiding principles and solid values linked to Christ's Word, thoughts and ways. The Holy Spirit will guide you in making ethical and moral decisions and making sound free will principle choices in all acts, as a part of deciding your faith and fate. The Source covers you in His grace and love and bestows goodness and mercy at your rear, while His glory is placed in your front. You will be led by the Lord in the fullness of His provisions, protection and prosperity along the path of life's journey. You are not simply born on earth to die unknown or of old age. Instead, you were born to travel in the power of the Creator and Source's spoken Word. God's has the authority to speak power at a thing and into a person, breaking shackles and loosening chains that are holding them down and back. This is accomplished through His infinitive power of equipping you to live on the divine path before the Creator and Source. As you live in each moment and every step taken along the journey of life, favor will follow you. *"And if you walk in obedience to me and keep my decrees and commands as David your father did, I will give you a long life."* (1 Kings 3:14)

The art of living is in the "I Am", for this is the Creator's name unto Himself, by Himself. Thereby, you must be attached to God, whose name is "I Am", "Jehovah", and "Emmanuel". He is the vital essence for all things, as in all things to the one He created. God took a portion of His divine nature, His spirit, upon which He laid your soul in the palm of His hand. Then, the Lord wrapped the two spiritual embryotic parts of life, your spirit and soul, to become one with the Creator and the Source. With your soul wrapped in the spirit of His divine nature, He blew His breath of life into His creation to give your heart life, and mind with Heavenly energy. He shaped you in His likeness for His purpose and completion of assignments at appointed times. Then, in the twinkling of a star's brightness, your life's journey began.

The Source was crystal clear, and laser focused in the Scriptures, *"No one comes to the Father, except through Me, for I Am, the Way, the Truth and the Life." (John 14:6)* God spoke through the prophets in the Old Testament and that which He spoke and promised has been fulfilled by Him unto the Covenants. That which Jesus Christ commanded to the apostles in the New Testament Scriptures must be remembered, meditated on, shared as the Good News, and introduced as the Gospel of Jesus Christ as the fulfilling of the new Covenant. This new covenant was founded on better promises, which is a binding agreement with the conditions for God to love you and the love of the Son Jesus Christ to be with you always. He alone is your Intercessor and Chief High Priest. You must observe and embrace being looked upon as the called mature disciple in Christ and that all are connected to the vine, who believes. The season is at hand in experiencing the quickening virtues and anointing of the Holy Spirit operating and manifesting in all Christians, in spirit, heart, mind, body and soul.

"Then Job replied to the Lord: "I know that you can do all things;
no purpose of yours can be thwarted. You asked, "Who is this that
obscures my plans without knowledge?" Surely, I did not understand,
things too wonderful for me to know." (Job 42:1-3)

ANTIDOTE 8 |
YOU WERE WORTH IT ALL

"He is the vital essence for all things, in all things to the one He created." Erogies Grigley Jr.

Are you out of a personal relationship with the Source and Creator, and do not know what to do? Being in a right relationship with God is to believe and know the Redeemer Jesus Christ. There is no other way to understand who you are and why you are worthy of God's faithfulness, grace, mercy and love. You should not have a spirit of fear, for this lack of faith is only for unbelievers. God did not give His children a spirit of fear, rather a sound mind and a strong spirit, filled with the Holy Spirit, to be an overcomer and victorious. *"I am the way, and the truth and the light. No one comes to the Father except though me." (John 14:6)*

God is the essential and vitality of the one He created. God is Sovereign in His divinity with a connection to our souls, which He desires to hold near His bosom. The Lord looked upon the waters and saw His face, thereby creating in His likeness your spiritual embryo to become one with the Source and Creator. Your soul, as a believer, takes on His divine nature because you allow the indwelling of His Spirit into His creation, to form your character. Have a renewed mind, renewed spirit to give your heart life, shaped in His likeness, for His purpose and appointed time. When your earthly life ends, your destiny begins Heavenly in spirit and truth before The Source and The Creator. God is true to all His promises, as promised the gift of salvation, to live the fullness of life spiritually and eternally. The Source remains faithful and the only path to the Creator, throughout the Scriptures. *"For there is one God and one mediator between God and mankind, the man Christ Jesus, who gave himself as a ransom for all people. This has now been witnessed to at the proper time." (1 Timothy 2:5-6)*

This declaration is a personal choice; to be in or out of relationship as "I am" with "I Am that I Am", and His only begotten Son, Jesus Christ, which are the headship of the royal family, which includes you. The complexity is not made simple, if and when you use your carnal mind, rational thinking, scientific references, and worldly influencing to make personal choices and ethical decisions, void of the Lord. You should choose humility as you see self; insight of your capacity in the Lord, and foresight of the plans God has for the special you. You truly are seen marvelous in His sight, filled with great faith and believing in great hope for tomorrow and the seasons forthcoming, with the sincerest gratitude that you can engender under His favor and love. Remember, your great works pleasing before the Lord will result in gifts and rewards awaiting you in Heaven, while blessings and favors await you on earth. Pay the price and incur the cost to serve the Source and Creator, worthy of every part of your being.

The price – a paid in full ransom by The Source, for the remainder of your earthly and eternal days, to be with Him in paradise and live with Him one day spiritually in His new city, called Zion, where you will know the full measure of being a part of royalty.

The cost – required obedience and discipline from you for the remainder of your days in *the art of living*, which the benefits and perks outweigh heavily and broadly, for such a brief period of time on this earth. *"He provided redemption for his people; he ordained his covenant forever-- holy and awesome is his name." (Psalm 111:9)*

Beloved, know that you are not alone. God will never place more on your character than you can bear. You have always been attached to God, whose name is "I Am That I Am", the Creator. Live spiritually and righteously, being holy as the Source, glorious and pleasing in the spiritual connection to Jesus Christ, whose name is "Wonderful".

His Will is for your will and ways to convert to His, for your purpose on earth, in spirit and manifesting by obedience in physical deeds and results. Out of darkness, from nothing, God the Creator and Jesus Christ the Source created the cosmos and humankind and the breath of life into him for joy and companionship. Then, the Creator rested, for He was pleased with His creation. As you reach a mature age to form your right personal decisions and good choices, you will realize that you not only have the power through the Holy Spirit to overcome, but you can help others in their difficulties.

The abundance of life's treasures is in the Triune God and spiritual relationship of covenant fellowship with the one He called His own, and with whom He is well pleased! It is a great deal, that Jesus first loved you and loved you so much, that He was willing to do anything in His Father's Will for you! God took a portion of His divine glory, upon which He gave to be the protector of your soul, becoming one with the Source and Creator. *"Whoever believes in me, as Scripture has said, rivers of living water will flow from within them." (John 7:38)*

His divine power is the connection to everything you need for a holy character and spiritual abundant life, for your purpose on earth and in Heaven for God's Will. The surrendered believer who share a spiritual relationship with the Source will be with both Christ and God. You will receive the fertile knowledge, sage wisdom and spiritual miraculous powers of the glorious One, the Son Jesus Christ. He is the only One able to give grace and mercy to your prayers, for the prayers of others and hope for a better tomorrow. By your belief, connection and daily communion with the

Source, you are able to overcome conforming to the patterns of the world that cover the earth and smother humanity in darkness and evilness.

The Source enables you to make the most of your time, in each season of your journey. You must recognize His hand along the path of living, as He transforms and renews your mind and spirit. We know that there are many temptations to challenge us from the angel Lucifer, and his plight is never ending. However, Jesus provides strength to overcome and a way of escape from these entrapments and snares.

Believers with great faith persevere along the path in their journey, as Christ's love is agape, good, pleasing, unconditional, perfect and without end. The Creator and Source knew you before you were formed in your mother's womb, as you came from the Creator as a spiritual being. In this walk as a disciple, transcend logic and rationale, to embrace a spiritual enlightenment to lead you along a path with a destiny to guarantee the spirit and soul, void of flesh, your return to the Source and Creator. (Jeremiah 1:5)

As you understand the Source's Will for your existence, He will pour forth His anointing to strengthen you. In all matters of existence in life, one must have a set of principles and values linked to Christ's thoughts and ways. You must be led by the Spirit to guide and lead you in making ethical decisions and making sound choices in all acts of faith and trust. The Source is your covering along life's highway to ensure your protection and rewards. It is completely up to you to determine what kind of personal relationship you have with Jesus Christ.

What about you? Are you satisfied and full of joy to know what it means to live in a journey with purpose in *the art of living* for Christ because of what He willingly did and does for you? *"In the days of His flesh, He offered up both prayers and supplications with loud crying and tears to the One able to save Him from death, and He was heard because of His piety." (Hebrews 5:7-10)*

Are you willing to incur and suffer the required costs? The costs and sacrifices carried over from the initial price paid for freedoms, liberties and favors on the path along your personal journey will determine your place in life and with the Lord, now and at your destiny. When you look into the mirror of life, you should be able to see God and the Son Jesus Christ, who created you in their likeness and poured out the glory of His Spirit into your being. You must be convinced that the Creator and the Source are one and through their divine power, you are connected to all of Heaven and share in His adoption. As you were joined in spirit to the Source, by belief, trust and faith, you are empowered to prevail and be victorious over the patterns of this dark world. In the Source, you are able to rise above and go through the storms of life liken to an eagle soaring in flight. With Jesus, you are given power to even change the tempest on the lake, that when the storm begins to rage, you are at peace with the Source, to whom even the winds obey.

The declaration to be in or out of a personal relationship with the Sovereign Will of Christ is a personal choice. You should desire and strive to be one with the headship of the royal family, which includes you, the adopted heir to the kingdom. You must resist to making choices that are non-spiritual and contrary to the Word of God and the deity of Jesus Christ. You should choose humility and have a servant attitude as you see self, for the insight needed to increase your capacity of faith and trust in the Lord, and exercise foresight of the plans God has for you. You truly are seen in God's sight as a beloved joy, if you are filled with great faith and believe with a great hope that all tomorrows and the seasons forthcoming are under God's control.

Approach each day in Christ with the Holy Spirit, and sincere gratitude of gratefulness that can resonate and be engendered, leading you to be in His favor, love, authority and power. This will enable Him to cover you with the grace and anointing of the Most High God. Know that your great works, coupled with your great faith is found pleasing before the Lord and will result in spiritual gifts released on earth and glorious rewards awaiting you in Heaven. Blessings and favors shall cover you and your children for generations upon generations to come, on earth, and in Heaven. Pay the price and incur the cost, by surrendering fully to Jesus Christ, for the decision to submit is worth all of your being.

The art of living well is in the "I Am", for this is the Creator's name unto Himself, by Himself. God has blown His divine spirit upon your soul, which He held in the palm of His hand. You must observe and be looked upon as the mature disciple in Christ, and freely be connected to the vine in spirit and truth. This free will to serve and reverence Him gives way to increase your soul's delight in the Lord, to stay focused on changing what is in your power and in giving all other matters and issues to the Lord. Jesus Christ finds favor with you for your discipline, pleasing works, great faith, zealous committed prayers and battle readiness. For you are a mature disciple worthy for preservation and receiving the prize and rewards of a loving Savior. Worship and praise God daily through thy lips and heart, knowing that the Father and Son sits on the throne of Righteousness and the Mercy Seat, as He surrounds you with love, peace and joy. *"Let us then approach God's throne of grace with confidence, so that we may receive mercy and grace to help us in our time of need." (Hebrews 4:16)*

There must be an experience of the quickening virtues and anointing of the Holy Spirit operating and manifesting in all Christians, by spirit, heart, mind and character. Your soul's delight should be in the Lord and outwardly professing and performing pleasing works unto the Lord, by a great measure of faith. Your aim and belief as a submitted spirit knows that the battle is truly worth the victory of loving Jesus Christ, while worshipping God the Father.

"In a loud voice they were saying: "Worthy is the Lamb,
who was slain, to receive power and wealth and wisdom and strength and
honor and glory and praise!" (Rev 5:12)

ANTIDOTE 9 |
YOU ARE SECOND IN LIFE

"The total surrender and acceptance as a child of God comes with unimaginable blessings and favor, spiritual and gifting characteristics, yielding blossoms and bearing divine fruits."
Erogies Grigley Jr.

Why do you find it hard to surrender to Christ and accept being in the center of His perfect Will? The surrender and acceptance that you are a child of God, comes with exceptional perks and benefits. These rewards come with the requirements of responsibility, discipline, trust and faith as the criterion to your Christian lifestyle for access to the distinct privileges from God. Only through humility, a contrite spirit and genuine love can a heart surrender to Christ. *"The Lord your God will circumcise your hearts and the hearts of your descendants, and you will love Him with all your heart and all your soul, so that you may live." (Deuteronomy 30:6)*

The art of living is in the divine blossoms of love, obedience, faith, wisdom and understanding from the Holy Spirit. These character traits and principles are Heavenly, spiritual and divine in the glorious spiritual nature of God and His desire for your life. You must become fully and indelibly cemented in your importance to God and the Source, for your will as one in His, for your life, purpose and journey. You must highly value your life as the first fruit of God, with a promise and covenant to be of great and grand significance in the earth's management, operation, evolution and balance. Understanding of your spiritual DNA (Distinguishing Notable Attributes) – talents and abilities to perform and Genetic Code – how God made you and how you are wired to feel, think and act, will help with strengthening your foundation and understanding your relationship with others, which we will discuss later in this book.

The gifting characteristics of identity and humility in Christ will yield blossoms to bear the divine fruits of love, joy, peace, faith, hope, kindness and fulfilling. Having Godly character is to bring joy to self, uplift others and glorify God the Father, Jesus Christ the Son and the Holy Spirit. You must feel, know, see and say, "I am" a child of the Most High God and kneel before the Holy One, Jesus Christ. You are an extraordinary creation, who was made a little lower than angels, but given divine dominion authority on earth and over the world. You are a spiritual warrior equipped with the full armor of God to be victorious in all challenges and battles: righteousness, truth, faith, peace and hope! As you reverence the King, the Savior, you also embrace the free gift of adoption into His spiritual family and the inheritances of God. You are wonderfully and marvelously made, a spectacular creation and peculiar strength in the power of the Source, through the Holy Spirit, with dominion authority and His power.

If you do not value and respect yourself, as only one knows oneself, much less than God knows one, you are no good to yourself or to your circle of life. Most people err in their ignorance and oblivious nature to the power of God that is within their reach and control. When you come into enlightenment of what is in your sphere of control and what is not, a mindset shifts to a higher level intellectually, intuitively, morally and spiritually. With this enlightenment, you believe others will understand what discipline and empowerment they have within themselves. You should embrace and live these enlightenments that incompetent and incompatible persons have no power over your true inner power and self. For in this power, the Creator keeps balance on earth and in life, for the enlightened to enjoy greater peace, joy, happiness and harmony; thereby fulfilling *the art of living*. *"Then make my joy complete by being like-minded, having the same love, being one in spirit and of one mind. Do nothing out of selfish ambition or vain conceit. Rather, in humility value others above yourselves, not looking to your own interests but each of you to the interests of the others." (Philippians 2:2-4)*

If you refuse to be second to God and Christ, you intentionally become a little god and less important to God, creating unacceptable high risks for being out of God's Will, grace and covering, without love. If you are in His Will, you can expect the favor of the Lord to be upon you in life for being girded, equipped, trained and resourced by God. You will be given an increase in knowledge, wisdom, understanding and favor to take the best care of self and not forfeit an abundant life in the art of living. Your arrogance and overt pride in an attempt to make yourself a little god will surely cause the evasiveness of joy and a fulfilled heart.

For this reason, as you may have heard of, you must pray steadfastly for one another to continuously ask the Source for the infilling of the Holy Spirit and revealing of the Source's Will for your life. The spiritual anointing of knowledge, wisdom, understanding and power for His Will to be done can only be given through the Holy Spirit. You must embrace obedience and commitment to purpose and cause in all your ways, discipline, sacrifices, and attitude. You must begin with new mornings, midnights, visions, dreams, talents, gifts and learning to reach for higher aspirations and sharing your good news stories and experiences, as testimonies. These tenants give strength to others to overcome their challenges, giants, despair, hopelessness and storms in life. When you are just and righteous, you move the heart of God, through selfless deeds and committed surrender to His perfect Will. *And the God of all grace, who called you to his eternal glory in Christ, after you have suffered a little while, will himself restore you and make you strong, firm and steadfast. To him be the power for ever and ever. Amen." (1 Peter 5:10-11)*

There is always the vision of glory on your disciple led, sacrificed and sanctified life. Your agape love is founded in the spiritual and favored relationship with God and Jesus Christ, by which you are justified and given grace. However, you rarely share your stories of testing, failures, suffering, trials or tattered shoes walked in with others. God appreciates the one who embraces *the art of living well* and adorns you with a visible halo above your walk. Also, you are filled with the spiritual anointing of Jesus Christ and His abundant grace. You must learn to embrace humility, deny self, reverence the Lord, exhort others and believe that God is no respecter of person. For it is He who sees your daily sacrifices and good works and hears your fervent and steadfast prayers. Specifically, pray for those who are sick, hurting, poor, homeless, hungered, widows, orphans and unjustly treated. Praying for these people should be first, then at the end of your prayer, ask the Lord to remember you and give you wisdom and joy of heart for another day to meet your needs and let you bring Him pleasure and the Father glory.

I am reminded of my wife's grandmother, Pauline Walker Brown's strong mindset and spirit, while sitting on her screened front porch of a "happy and strong" framed house. She gave everyone wisdom for humility, tapered with courage and responsibility, in the Source and Creator. She said to me, "Grig, always remember: it's a poor frog who won't praise his own pond. Shame on him, for others will praise their own pond."

I concluded this powerful quote to mean, "In the sight of God, family and friends, remember to be thankful and grateful unto God for who you are and what little or much you may have. Be content where you are and with what you have, for it is yours. You are only as great as you honor the Lord, belief in self, help others, give of self, and live to please the Lord, first and always!" I have strived daily to live for Christ and family, for friends and to change some enemies. Some days with great difficulty; some days having stumbled and fallen, but constantly rising with the Lord's hand. In doing so, you will find humility and strength with gratitude and great thanks in praising God for deliverance and safekeeping.

There are many simple reasons and yet critical things, low and high moments and treasured and forgetful experiences to give God praise and worship. Thereafter, you will find joy of having a home with a loving and honorable family and being able to help those less fortunate to find restoration and hope. This is important, for all have drifted afloat in life at one point or another, and perhaps drifting or weaving off the path of *the art of living well* along one's journey.

It is my desire to speak to you as you read the 33 Antidotes and expository food for life, to pass along various inner perspective and positive subconscious thoughts, spiritual uplifts and Heavenly gifts so that you can be strengthened, by speaking to yourself. My desire is for the quotes, Antidotes and Scriptures poured out from within me from the Lord to mutually encourage you during your reading. And, when we greet each other at a book signing or social media, you will feel we know each other as friends in Christ. We must be encouraged by the faithfulness and testimonies of each other, in your triumphs over giants, your rebound and rise above failures, and your moments of miracles from defeat, as well mine, for which the Lord joined us together for a time such as this.

"Let us hold unswervingly to the hope we profess, for he who promised is faithful. And let us consider how we may spur one another on toward love and good deeds, not giving up meeting, as some are in the habit of doing, but encouraging one another – and all the more as you see the Day approaching." (Hebrews 10:23-25)

ANTIDOTE 10 |
KNOW YOUR ROYALTY

"I live with the fullness of liberties, freedoms and harmony to make simple the complex and difficulties of life." Erogies Grigley Jr.

Have you ever asked yourself, 'Who am I?' Do you know who you are – where you came from – in spirit and soul? How was your complex mind, organs, bodily system designed? What lineage are you a part of? To know who you are, you must first discover to Whom you belong and where you came from. Not only this, but you must know where you are going in this life and life after death. Many people go through life without a defined identity and purpose and give no thought to the future beyond their fleshly bodies. *"I am the Lord your God, who brought you up out of Egypt. Open wide your mouth and I will fill it." (Psalm 81:10)*

To make simple the complex and difficult, the illustration used is a comparison between sheep and goats. The Lord refers to sheep as His children, but goats are referred to as those that do not believe in Him and who He will not let have any part in His kingdom. As redeemed people under grace, sanctified and justified through Christ's works, sufferings, death, resurrection and ascension into Heaven, you have been delivered and redeemed with a new standard and deeper meaning for living abundantly. As believers in Christ, Christians are raised to a new spiritual dimension and righteous standing in Jesus Christ. He no longer views us as sheep but calls us His friends and recognizes us as His adopted children to God His Father. *"Then the LORD God formed a man from the dust of the ground and breathed into his nostrils the breath of life, and the man became a living being. Now the LORD God had planted a garden in the east, in Eden; and there he put the man he had formed." (Genesis 2:7-8)*

As an adopted child into the royal family, you are now a shepherd for caring for His sheep (the saved) and leading goats (worldly, unsaved and people who lost their way) to Christ. You are the chosen one given the Spirit of Christ to become better, stronger, wiser and richer in love, joy, humility and charity for living an abundant life on earth, and through great works have rewards awaiting you in Heaven. You are also given the awesome assignment of making better those who need help and salvation for an abundant life today and in Heaven tomorrow. *"Before I formed you in the womb, I knew you, before you were born, I set you apart." (Jeremiah 1:5)* Through love and compassion, you can lead the saved and unsaved into a relationship with each other, so they can live more peaceful, joyous and abundant lives. You can also discover your beauty and strength through a caring, nurturing and giving heart and mind. Your mission must be to lead people selflessly and humbly to Jesus Christ for a new identity. Also, teach people to enter into a growing relationship with Christ as their Lord and Savior, and God the Father as adopted heirs of His kingdom family, on earth and in Heaven.

You will go through the filtering process of assessing life's negative and positive experiences to see, learn and understand the conflicts and circumstances of your desires. Conflict and circumstances are not only needed in life but are necessary and sure to come. Some conflicts help you to hone and strengthen yourself and others in your circle, to build courage and the will to fight spiritually, as needed, to protect self, family and community. It is worth reinforcing that the essence of a successful life is in your ability to control things within your power and existence, influenced by God's will to command submission, at will and on the ready! Many things are spiritual, of which you have the promises of God, and full control if you allow Christ to operate sovereignly over your spirit. What you think, what you ruminate upon, what you surge forth as an opinion or thought, what you choose consciously or subconsciously in desire and objectivity is within the sphere of your control, by your will. If you reduce your earthly and worldly desires, the less these desires will stir inside your mind for finding satisfaction and becoming a large playground of mental gymnastics of defeating thoughts. We can have thoughts for things that do not exist, or challenges to the mind's amygdala to raise force field shields and deceive one of impending danger, when there is actually beauty, peace and love in old familiar colors, sounds, fragrances and signs. *"Christ said to you and God, but to which of the angles has He ever said, 'Sit at My right hand, until, I make your enemies a footstool for your feet?'" (Hebrews 1:13)*

When you become learnt in the way of the Samurai, the lesser the desires to acquire control, increases greater control one has to will one's spiritual and mental strength to accomplish great physical feats by the Lord's strength. If the desires grow stronger, so too will the control to use your assets to gain the identified desires of opportunities – usually physical and material, as well emotionally, mentally and spiritually. If you understand and subdue your desires, such as things that are harmful, distracting or that belong to another person, the less misunderstandings will arise, and you will not find fault with the other. But the cycle of mental and carnal desires become fleshly, repeated and leads you down a destructive path, for pain, ruin and heartbreak. For some, they experience loss and even death of a loved one or committing suicide. Our societies have become engulfed in capitalism and creation of hate and false fleeting desires as a norm in life, and prey on giving satisfaction and happiness of false things not needed, by advertising and promoting increased happiness through direct spending – while not valuing the dollar for self. This cycle is not only ongoing but is transferred to your children when they are merely a few years old. Thus, the capitalistic and false appeal to be a part of capitalism and materialism in society through ownership and bragging continues, without any end in sight.

Draw close to living a life filled with the spirit, not in flesh that focuses on the needs, wants and challenges of the world. For the world rises to take all into its grasp and draw every ounce of energy, every fiber of their being, every possession – even children and family members, and every breath from your body, if you submit to the world's ways. Living in spiritual harmony with self, humanity, and the universe of life through the Source and the Creator shows unseen and unheralded wonders from Heaven. A spirit-filed abundant life simply cannot be discovered and experienced from a blissful and morbid black and white worldly perspective. There is a way to live abundantly, in full harmony and complete peace with self, surroundings and within the inhabitants of the earth. You must choose to live above the life you were dealt and realize that the Lord is your Creator who has great compassion, forgiveness, hope for a future and divine care for your life. The Lord has planned a life for you to prosper and to find longevity through His spirit, not for you to be harmed. *"My frame was not hidden from you when I was made in the secret place, when I was woven together in the depths of the earth. Your eyes saw my unformed body; all the days ordained for me were written in your book before one of them came to be." (Psalm 139: 15-16)*

The Lord knew you before you were formed in your mother's womb and set you a part through His grace and love. When Adam was formed in the Garden, Scripture gives a clear picture of how you were created and the purpose for which the Lord made provisions for you. The Lord formed man first, followed by woman, originating from good soil that the Lord had created in the Garden, which was a part of Heaven. Before, man's initial existence was simply a formed and lifeless clump of clay, until the Lord blew His breath of life into him. That is, His Spirit into man; and also, into woman. This marvelous and divine act created living beings with creative and infinite good thoughts and free will spirits. Your soul is not separated from the Spirit of God, but loved by the Lord. *"For this reason, since the day we heard about you, we have not stopped praying for you. We continually ask God to fill you with the knowledge of his will through all the wisdom and understanding that the Spirit gives, so that you may live a life worthy of the Lord..." (Colossians 1:9-10)*

Both man and woman, known as Adam and Eve, were given complete dominion over the Garden of Eden in which they were placed in by God. They were assigned to cultivate and manage their Garden home with assistance from angels on special assignment. God created all in spirit and soul in Heaven, before any were conceived in the flesh through mother and father on earth.

God expects the same in your home, where you have complete authority to rule and keep His commandments. As a believer, you are part of the Spirit of God and tethered to Him through Jesus Christ, unto whom all were and will be redeemed. Although you were born in the flesh on earth, earth is not your home but is rather a temporary dwelling place to carry out the purpose of God which He placed on your life. The physical earth, in your physical body is not your permanent home to dwell, nor the permanent fleshly home for your spirit. As your flesh shall fade away and die, your spirit can live with God forever in a new earth, which is Heavenly, where the Lord Jesus will reign as King. He will restore the original Garden of Eden to the Heavenly place He created for all of His creations, especially His awesome creation made of Himself in image and likeness, man and woman, as His children.

"However, as it is written: "What no eye has seen, what no ear has heard, and what no human mind has conceived" – the things God has prepared for those

who love him – these are the things God has revealed to us by his Spirit. The Spirit searches all things, even the deep things of God. For who knows a person's thoughts except their own spirit within them? In the same way no one knows the thoughts of God except the Spirit of God." (1 Corinthians 2:9-11)

ANTIDOTE 11 |
IS YOUR LIFE SIFTED
OR SHIFTED?

"His Sovereignty loves beyond what we can see, imagine or think."
Erogies Grigley Jr.

Have you doubted Christ's love? Have you ever gone without food or a roof over your head, not knowing what would happen through the night, let alone the next morning? You should not worry about the things of tomorrow or in the world, for a believer's strength is not in knowing the future but in knowing the One who holds the future in His hands. *"Do not be like them, for your Father knows what you need before you ask him." (Matthew 6:8)*

There are provisions, peace and perseverance in Christ, through God, in our desire and quest to survive, live abundantly and have power over evilness in the world. For we are God's empowered children who He loves beyond what we can see, imagine or think. It is wonderful that our ways and thoughts are not God's thoughts and ways. We are abiding in His secret place daily where He alone hides us under His wings of protection and prepare provisions of manna and living waters for our spirits, minds, hearts, bodies and souls. *I know what it is to be in need, and I know what it is to have plenty. I have learned the secret of being content in any and every situation, whether well fed or hungry, whether living in plenty or in want. I can do all this through Christ who gives me strength." (Philippians 4:12-13)*

Our Lord and Messiah, Jesus Christ not only hears the righteous prayers, petitions and cries but will prove to meet your every need, with your good works, out of His grace and mercy, which are His promises, in His Will as Mediator. He does require you to be obedient and to trust His Word and to love one another while showing compassion and goodwill. Be obedient through great works, Fruit of the Spirit, faithfulness and a living testimony to others, in love, for Him alone. *"When I am with the Gentiles who do not follow the Jewish law, I too live apart from that law so I can bring them to Christ. But I do not ignore the law of God; I obey the law of Christ. To the weak I became weak, to win the weak. I have become all things to all people so that by all possible means I might save some. I do all this for the sake of the gospel that I may share in its blessings." (1 Corinthians 9:21-23)*

Are you being robbed of love by people and waiting on Jesus Christ to love you? You should not seek love but find love in the gaze of the eyes and affair of the heart in spirit, and a personal relationship with Jesus Christ. For therein, love will find you and stir your soul. *"There is no fear in love. But perfect love drives out fear, because fear has to do with punishment. The one who fears is not made perfect in love. We love because he first loved us. Whoever claims to love God yet hates a brother or sister is a liar. For whoever does not love their brother and sister, whom they have seen, cannot love God, whom they have not seen. And he has given us this command: Anyone who loves God must also love their brother and sister." (1 John 4:18-21)*

You must intentionally and premeditatedly pause each day, set aside Heavenly 'me time', and slow down to be attentive to see you as the wonderful and glorious marvelous person Christ created for His good pleasure and the Father's glory. Also, listen intently with your conversations with God, for He is full of love and desires to lead you to your husband or wife, and covenant friends who He chose to give love and support to you, just as you are, where you are. But you must incline more than your ear to hear. You must enter into the spirit realm and open your heart to receive, while looking for signs and wonders in your mind from visions and dreams He gives. God will be true, for it is His greatest desire for man and woman to marry and become as one. The institution of marriage is where you are adopted into His Heavenly family and help build the kingdom of God for His glory and existence. *"Jesus replied: 'Love the Lord your God with all your heart and with all your soul and with all your mind.'" (Matthew 22:37)*

Understand Christ's love for you and ponder on what He freely did, gave up and sacrificed for you to be loved by Him and the Father. This was no small or large task. It was an impossible mission which only Jesus Christ could re-establish for His children, by first reconciling them to Himself, through suffering, crucifixion and death. God promised He would raise Jesus Christ from death and give Him full dominion, power and authority over you as His own redeemed adopted child, along with the power over the world and heaven. What a blessing. What a joy. God and His Son chose you to love. He loves you in spite of anything! *"The LORD directs the steps of the godly. He delights in every detail of their lives. Though they stumble, they will never fall, for the LORD holds them by the hand. I was young and now I am old... For the LORD loves justice, and he will never abandon the godly. He will keep them safe forever..." (Psalm 37:23-29)*

Is your life being sifted or shifted? Are you being robbed of abundant living by your choices, certain people and the inability to say 'No' when called upon? *"But you are not like that, for the Holy One has given you his Spirit, and all of you know the truth. So I am writing to you not because you don't know the truth but because you know the difference between truth and lies. And who is a liar? Anyone who says that Jesus is not the Christ is both foolish and ignorant. Anyone who denies the Father and the Son will not inherit the kingdom of heaven. Anyone who denies the Son doesn't have the Father, either. But anyone who acknowledges the Son has the Father also." (1 John 2:20-23)*

Take inventory of who you are, what you do in a day and who you have invited into your life. Now, mark an 'X' for deleting, next to the person, thing, or event that is sifting value (i.e. time, money, joy, peace) from your life. Next, mark a 'K' for keeping, next to the person, thing, or event that adds value to your life and that you plan to keep. Most importantly, make a plan to release the sifters from your life. This will leave you with valuable people and things to positively work together to shift your life into living the full and abundant life. *"But now you also, put them all aside: anger, wrath, malice, slander, and abusive speech from your mouth. Do not lie to one another..., a renewal in which there is no distinction between Jews and Greeks." (Colossians 3:8-10)*

Remember, prayer is to become personal with Christ and become powerful, instead of being powerless. Through fervent and effectual prayer, you can be assured of your faith and trust being manifested in your heart's desires with Christ. Be cautious, though. You may find some of the shifters' risks far exceeds the rewards, and you must remove them or the action, which is not in His will. Changing your environment, people, actions and things will lead to a change in perspective and attitude, which is required to enrich your life. Take accountability for your decisions so you can make room for *the art of living well*. Sometimes, you must say 'No' and leave the emotions of 'Yes' in the spiritual discernment from the inner self that gives the wisdom and strength to say 'No'. Learn to drop Lot, as did Abraham, when strife, pain, anxiety and selfishness with vain conceited people invade your space. Then, after dropping Lot, God will hear and speak to you, with blessings and prosperity. *"So Abraham said to Lot, 'let's not have any quarreling between you and me...Is not the whole land before you? Now separate yourself from me. If you go to the left, I will go to the right. If you go to the right, I will go to the left...'" (Genesis 13:8-9)*

Why are you doing just enough to get by, enough to satisfy the boss, people – yet you want more? Colossians 3:12-17 reads, *"So, as those who have been chosen of God, holy and beloved, put on a heart of compassion, kindness, humility, gentleness and patience; bearing with one another, and forgiving each other... Let the word of Christ richly dwell within you, with all wisdom teaching and admonishing one another...singing with thankfulness in your hearts to God. Whatever you do in word or deed, do all in the name of the Lord Jesus, giving thanks through Him to God the Father."*

When you learn to say 'No', you will see changes in environment, deletion of phone numbers, falling away of certain people and separation from foolishness and vain living. Then, Christ will fill your voids with His desired blessings and meet all your needs and heart's desires. Let not your prayers go silent before the Lord! *"Then the LORD appeared to Solomon at night and said to him, I have heard your prayer and have chosen this place for Myself as a house of sacrifice. If I shut up the heavens... and My people who are called by My name humble themselves and pray and seek My face and turn from their wicked ways, then I will hear from heaven, will forgive their sin and will heal their land. For now, I have chosen and consecrated this house that My name may be there forever..."* (2 Chronicles 7:12-17)

These are the times your patience, faith and trust must be absolute for rekindling your relationship with Christ. For in this relationship rests spiritual opportunities, to be manifested in solutions and by changing the life you are currently living, but for God. If you belong to Christ, you who are called by His name, you must humble yourself, pray sincerely with a repentant heart and contrite spirit for God to move in your life. Stop venting, drop the little gods and men, seek Christ's face and His heart, and turn from your worldly and wicked ways; then Christ will hear from Heaven with a moved heart of mercy and grace. Where He will forgive your sins and disappointments for your whole house, heal and restore and expand your territories with favor and His Will. *"As for you, if you walk before Me as your father David walked, even to do according to all that I have commanded you, and will keep My statutes and My ordinances, then I will establish your royal throne..."* (1 Kings 9:4)

Jesus has given us all of Himself, which is to give all of God. For in the beginning, Jesus was the Word, which God spoke into existence. He sat at the right hand of God, as the Mercy Seat for humanity. Yet, He was one with God, as God birthed Jesus from His own Spirit. God sent Him as a ransom to pay the price for His endless creations, who was made in His likeness and image. Therefore, Jesus was able to give a new covenant, founded on better and greater promises, which were on the foundation of God's given authority and power in Heaven and on earth.

"A new command I give you: Love one another.
As I have loved you, so you must love one another." (John 13:34)

ANTIDOTE 12 |
DISCOVER THE SOURCE

"As long as the branches are connected to the vines of the tree,
the potential is high that they will bear fruit. So, too,
is the relationship between the Lord's greatest creation, humankind."
Erogies Grigley Jr.

Do you find life difficult? Are you losing hope? Do you feel disconnected to Christ and love ones? Being lonely and not having a great relationship with a special someone can cause depression and a feeling of disconnection. This island outlook leaves one undiscovered by others, but also seeing life wounded, unwanted and lost to the wonder and awesomeness that awaits you in the Lord. *"Hope in the Lord and keep his way." (Psalm 37:34)*

There is a day when Christ will return and you who believe, who are faithful and do not weary or faint, shall reign with Him. You will never be dismissed from His sight for all eternity. You can enjoy this reign today, if you accept Jesus Christ through repentance and surrender to Him. You must seek forgiveness of sins and believe that God is His Father. With your personal faith in Him you have salvation. By confession from your heart and the belief that God raised Jesus from the dead, you can be connected to the Source. When you surrender your heart, Christ becomes your Lord and Savior and you become His friend and adopted heir into the Kingdom of God.

There is something special about making a public declaration that honors the Lord, as He said, *"If you are ashamed of me before people, I would be ashamed of you before My Father and no you shall not enter." (Mark 8:38)* Make the commitment to connect to Christ, your Source. If you have not, this is critical and can be the best day of your life by making the most important decision of your life. The roots of a broad tree and grape vines stretch wide and run deep, as wide as its branches and as deep as the depth to dip its tips in water. The branches that are connected to the tree and vine will bear much fruit. So, too is the relationship between the Lord's greatest creation, humankind. Stay connected to the Source and prepare for a bountiful harvest of life, bearing good fruit to share and Spiritual gifts to give. You must hold on to the truth that neither the Creator nor the Source are respecter of persons. They honor obedience and faithfulness to the Word and reverence to the Sovereign and Omnipotent God and Lord.

No one is born equally, neither physically nor spiritually. After you took the first breath of fresh air, you became a spirit, a living being and agent for God's divine Will and sole purpose. You must feel, know, see and speak "I am" through your spiritual DNA and initiate movement within your Genetic Code, which is connected to the Vine, the Source. The Creator and the Source took the soul, spirit and mind and formed thee into one. He flashed you from Heaven through time and space to earth. He clothed you in humanity, with a good heart and the appearance of flesh outwardly. You are designed with water and blood inwardly, and a conscious and subconscious mind spiritually. You are led by the spirit of free will choice which may move your heart into a closer relationship with God and the Son. Look around at the conditions that people are born in throughout the earth. People are born differently in the eyes of man and eyes of God. For God chooses who He wants to do His Will, to be born in abounding or born in abashing. We are all born, except one, the traitor and betrayer of Jesus Christ, to have a chance at salvation and God's glory eternally – where we will not be equal around the throne of grace and mercy. For all have come short of the glory of God! *"The years of my pilgrimage are a hundred and thirty. My years have been few and difficult, and they do not equal the years of the pilgrimage of my fathers." (Genesis 47:9)*

After you took the first breath of fresh air, you became a living spirit, a living being and agent for God's divine and perfect Will. To travel along His created path for life, in this journey that is connected with the Source infinitely and eternally. *The art of living well* is in the divine blossoms of spirit, truth and love that matures over time from buds, and finally into fruit to become ripened for the harvest and enjoyment. Galatians 5:22 record, *"But the fruit of the Spirit is love, joy, peace, forbearance, kindness, goodness, faithfulness, gentleness and self-control"*, by the love and faithfulness of Jesus Christ, our Lord, Master and Savior. There is a season for all things, but there should always be a time for kindness blossoms that spring forth love. Love is the essence of joy wrapped in the abundance of humility and forgiveness. This act is not easy but should be sincere and bountiful from the giver to the one in need and called friend. *"Let us go early to the vineyards to see if the vines have budded, if their blossoms have opened, and if the pomegranates are in bloom – there I will give you my love." (Song of Solomon 7:12)*

Through the Source, you possess the ability to yield divine blossoms of spirit and in truth and to bear a harvest to live a good, pleasing and abundant life. You freely choose to give and forgive in your quest to bear divine fruits of love. Or, you can choose the opposite of evil that surfaces every day. Be careful not to let ruin and hatred enter your thoughts and way of life! *"This day I call the heavens and the earth as witnesses against you that, I have set before you life and death, blessings and curses. Now choose life, so that you and your children may live, and that you may love the Lord your God..." (Deuteronomy 30:19)*

Living is in the divine blossoms of the spirit. You should live near the cherry blossoms along the path of life, uplift others and glorify God the

Father and the Son Jesus Christ. This lifestyle can only be accomplished through Jesus Christ the Son and the Holy Spirit. He leads us to fulfill His divine purpose, as He covers His favored people under His wings of protection. For your aim must be to strive to always be connected to the Source and in the center of God's Will, not that of your selfish will and fleeting vanity! For in this dilemma, the Lord only asks, "Do you believe", and "On this day, shall you choose life and not death, freely your decision?"

"Now it is God who makes both us and you stand firm in Christ.
He anointed us, set his seal of ownership on us, and put his
Spirit in our hearts as a deposit, guaranteeing what is to come."
(2 Corinthians 1:21-22)

ANTIDOTE 13 |
LET CHRIST REVEAL
HIS PURPOSE

"One can gleam light in life and pursue all of the promises of Christ."
Erogies Grigley Jr.

How can you not have abiding faith in Christ, with the fullness of the knowledge and understanding of the depth of His love for you? Faith is a word that comes your way, only if you can hear what is being said and you believe with a trusting spirit and heart. Faith is about believing and trusting in the person to have you in their best interest and heart. Faith in Christ is knowing that you are loved. You can trust Him, and your purpose will be revealed in His Will for your life. *"For I know the plans I have for you," declares the LORD, "plans to prosper you and not to harm you, plans to give you hope and a future." (Jeremiah 29:11)*

God desires all believers to enter into his realm through the invested dominion, power and authority placed in Christ in Heaven and on earth. Christ is the only answer for the salvation of humanity and to be our victor over defeating Satan. My friend, Christ cares for you deeply. He informs us that He knows the thoughts that He thinks towards you. These thoughts are of peace and prosperity, not harm or evil.

Therefore, as a seasoned believer or a new babe in Christ, your full belief and now faith in heart, mind, spirit and soul should be with a great hope in the Lord. You must exist to live in Christ and He in you. He encourages you each day to believe that you are His and you belong to the Father through Him. He will never abandon you in this life or the next, for Christ is of the Trinity which is the makeup of God. There can be no distinction in who God as the Father is, nor who Jesus as the Son of God is. If you have seen Christ, you also have done the same with God, for they are one. As a Christian, you cannot allow fear to come into your sphere of life. Although God judges, He gave Christ the power and authority to forgive. Therefore, you should marvel at His greatness and reverence in His holiness with all power over Satan and his deceiving followers. For Christ paid the price for redemption and salvation with His precious blood. In Him you have a sound mind and spiritual authority to rise above wickedness, confusion and unprofitable conversations. You can walk in Christ's power and might spiritually, manifested in the physical and be victorious in His glory.

When you believe, you can gleam light in life and pursue all of the promises of Christ and what God has purposed for you. God lets us know in the Scriptures that He makes it a point to know and keep track of every strand of hair on your head. He validates that there is nothing about you that is foreign to Him, even in illnesses, pains, and any condition which come upon you. Not only does He know what you are going through, but He is able to heal all manner of heartbreaks and sickness. He cares so deeply for you because you are His own child. He stores blessings, favors, and grace and mercies for you in heavenly storage vaults, for He knows your ways and shortcomings. You are His beloved adopted friend, in the heavenly family, for His love is all encompassing and exceeds any expectation you can imagine or think. *And the peace of God, which transcends all understanding, will guard your hearts and your minds in Christ Jesus."* *(Philippians 4:7)*

In order to move in Christ, your motives must first be right for His grace and assurance. Only through a pure heart can His glory be revealed to carryout Christ's purpose for your life. The Word of God must be firmly planted in your heart by the infilling of the Holy Spirit, forcing the fleeing from your own lustful and worldly desires. You must submit freely and totally to the Will of Christ and the Word of God, to produce a spiritual life that is pleasing unto the Lord. This gives you the anointing of His precious glory and full assurance that Christ's purpose for your life shall come to past and cannot return unto Him void. Your heart must be broken, spirit made contrite and soul purified before you can be used by Christ. All of your selfishness and sinful indulgences must be removed and destroyed from within the inner-person. Only then can you receive and understand Christ's purpose for your life and begin to allow the Holy Spirit to lead you into the spiritual life on earth, which He planned and desires for you.

His precepts and principles are put in place to build up the workings and duties of a loyal and disciplined disciple to do God's Will. Life is not about your will, but reflecting a total change in the old person by creation of the new person, in whom Christ says, "I am well pleased my good and faithful servant". In this life, in the journey along the path of living abundantly, you learn that all people are reflections of God's total creation – all are born, all will die. But, if you are a believer and keep the faith, dying is not the end of your journey. You must refrain from conducting foolish and vain conversations, thinking to be right, but not righteous in spiritual conduct and bearing no fruit for the Kingdom. Some even find themselves oblivious to acting as little gods, through self-centeredness, worshipping money and materialism, and power and fame. All of these are fleeting and short lasting. But praises be unto Christ the King of Kings, who is the Redeemer, and that all can be redeemed by the blood of Christ. *But just as he who called you is holy, so be holy in all you do…; 'Be holy, because I am holy…'." (1 Peter 1:15-17)*

My understanding has matured to realize that one's span of life, regardless of length or longevity, is that humankind's existence is relative. The balance of life is no different than the lily's, clovers and pansies in the fields. They are surrounded by green pastures in the Spring, which fades and withers away in the Fall and Winter months. God is the author and finisher of our faith and race. Only God gives increase through the planting of the Holy Spirit in our fleshly tabernacles to subdue our hearts, minds and thoughts. Stir up your heart and encourage your spirit to hear the Lord, to live humbly, and be obedient to love one another. Receive each other as they are, and where they are.

At any hour, all of us can wither like the flowers and the grass of the field. The difference is that our lives have an appointment with Christ, which is required through death. Even then, do no fear death. Instead, you must embrace dying as your purpose has been completed for the Will of God. Your spirit and soul are returning to Christ, as it was before the foundations of the earth were formed. This becomes your blessed joy, peace and treasure to lay hold on; to fear not, rather rejoice that your purpose is fulfilled. You have lived a good and glorious life, and now you shall see the glory of God and the treasure of His glory and rewards laid up in heaven for you, based on your obedience, worship, trust, praise, faith and good works.

God is an awesome Father and Lord, as He keeps all His promises and makes His purpose known for our lives, even when we do not deserve His goodness, grace and mercy. But, because we are His and He loved us first, as His favored and phenomenal creation, we will always be the blossoms He cares for, to sprout into the intended good fruit. *"Because God wanted to make the unchanging nature of his purpose very clear to the heirs of what was promised, he confirmed it with an oath. God did this so that, by two unchangeable things in which it is impossible for God to lie, we who have fled to take hold of the hope set before us may be greatly encouraged. We have this hope as an anchor for the soul, firm and secure. It enters the inner sanctuary behind the curtain, where our forerunner, Jesus, has entered on our behalf. He has become a high priest forever, in the order of Melchizedek." (Hebrews 6:17-20)*

It is important to realize there is a great hope that is attainable, and Christ's love is waiting for you to humble yourself and ask Him to enter into your heart. In Him, you can take refuge and solace with the full knowledge of trusting Him for all your needs. Be anxious for nothing in this world, but zealous for the grace, mercy and love of God. We will all have trials and tribulations, for we were born into a world of darkness and sin. But we are not alone, for the Father is with us through Jesus Christ and the wonderful Helper, to see us through all things. Therefore, pray unceasingly, and take heart in knowing that your sufferings are seen and will build the spiritual character necessary for you to have a firm foundation in the Lord. God will never leave you or forsake you, allowing you to be all alone. He is your glorious Creator and will always show up right on time to empower you with the strength of the Holy Spirit. As your faith increases, so will your trust in Christ. He will increase your wisdom and understanding and enlarge your territory. He will keep you abiding in His strength and cover you in His bountiful and unending love. Your roots will grow deep into God's love and keep you strong. *"I ask you, therefore, not to be discouraged because of my sufferings for you, which are your glory. For this reason, I kneel before the Father, from whom every family in heaven and on earth derives its name. I pray that out of his glorious riches he may strengthen you with power through his Spirit in your inner being, so that Christ may dwell in your hearts through faith. And I pray that you, being rooted and established in love, may have power, together with all the Lord's holy people, to grasp how wide and long and high and deep is the love of Christ, and to know this love that surpasses knowledge—that you may be filled to the measure of all the fullness of God. Now to him who is able to do immeasurably more that all we ask or imagine, according to his power that is at work within us, to him be glory…, for ever and ever! Amen." (Ephesians 3:13-21)*

Most people murmur and complain about not having enough. Some become jealous of their neighbor, and even share their jealousy about a family member who seems to live a more prosperous and fulfilling life. This is not the Will of the Lord, nor the way and thoughts of the Lord. Rather, the Lord is your provider and protector who enables you to have a spirit of contentment whether abounding or abasing. *"I know your deeds, that you are neither hot nor cold. I wish that you were one or the other! But since you are like lukewarm—neither hot nor cold—I am about to spit you out of my mouth! You say, 'I am rich; I have acquired wealth and do not need a thing.' But you do not realize that you are wretched, pitiful, poor, blind and naked." (Revelations 3:15-17)*

There are several ordinances that are recognized to keep us joined to Christ and to be performed as often as we choose to do them in remembrance of Him. We also exercise His laws for our individual communion and relationship with Christ. All of us desire a comfortable life, and when difficulty arises, we seek comfort in family, friends and lastly Christ. Many times, people out of alignment with Christ cannot find comfort, joy or peace because their motives and hearts are impure with wrongful purposes. Instead, draw on the strength and help of the Holy Spirit and push pride aside, trample on ego and lay aside vanity. These selfish cups may taste sweet but become sour to the stomach and lead to a life of grandeur and praise by the roar of the crowd. Learn that to be in a right relationship with Christ will not always be comfortable. However, the bitter cup cannot pass from one to whom God has purposed it, but together with Jesus Christ, the bitter cup can be turned into wine. If you join in a covenant and obedient relationship with Christ and enter into communion often with Christ in worship, praise, prayer and conversations, you will be in a right relationship.

Be encouraged to always tell people who are apt to listen that God is not a respecter of persons and does not show favoritism. *"Then Peter opened his mouth, and said, "Of a truth I perceive that God is no respecter of persons." (Acts 10:34)* But, He does honor obedience in doing His Will, which almost always involve servitude. The word 'servant' scares people away, as though it is belittling of a thing to do. On the contrary, servitude is the greatest gift, act or sign of righteousness and humility that gets the Lord's attention and moves His heart towards His servant disciple. The Lord said, *"Not so with you. Instead, whoever wants to become great among you must be your servant, and whoever wants to be first must be your slave – just as the Son of Man did not come to be served, but to serve, and to give his life as a ransom for many." (Matthew 20:26-28)*

When pursuit of greatness is put away, a great burden bearing on the spirit and soul is taken away. Folly must depart when Christ enters the doorway to one's heart and soul. If you are a true and noble disciple of Christ in the ministry of the Gospel, foolishness, quarrelling and mischief cannot stand or take root. Within the people of God, dwells the greater laborer and power. Disciples who are diligent, humble and wise seek only to do good and pleasing works. Good works unto God, Christ, the Holy Spirit and to their brother and sister in the love of the Spirit, that Christ will be honored. It is in these moments that the heart of the matter lives, which is to promote the Gospel's Good News of Jesus Christ and the salvation of souls. This is the light of life, which is living in the image and likeness of the Creator and the Source.

Christ's life was for all, the ransom price he paid was for all, and the separation cost from the Father and heaven's divinity was a sufficient ransom for the many souls - past, present and future. I asked Christ why I had to suffer 11 major surgeries in less than four-years. He responded, 'Why not you?! I chose you because I love you, and I made my own Son Christ suffer exceedingly greater than your minor sufferings, superior to that which any man will ever have to endure. Your sufferings are for My glory and testimonies of your tests to share with and help others overcome their trials and tests, while leading them to Me and increasing their faith." Only then did I stop my pity party. I embraced that not only was my sufferings for Christ, but also for preparing me to be wiser, stronger and better. I had a greater anointing in my life to do a great work for Christ and for His people. Thus, this book was written. *"I consider that our present sufferings are not worth comparing with the glory that will be revealed in us." (Romans 8:18)*

Always remember to be loving and embrace an attitude of servitude for all manner of people. Jesus Christ came not to abolish the law, but to fulfill all prophecies. He came to serve all that were heavily laden, stricken in sickness and illnesses, destitute, poor, widows and orphans, along with injustices and inequalities. His life and presence allow for all to be made equal in His eyes when they come into Paradise and the Kingdom with Him. A change in behavior and attitude starts as a child. I find younger people more eager than adults for a thirst and grasping of God's Word. Christ did not come to be served, nor to abolish the law, but rather to serve and to fulfill all prophecies and give God's children a new covenant, founded on better promises. I wonder how the Lord wrestled with the many dynamics, personalities, motives and jockeying for position which promoted disputes amongst the disciples? They all wanted to be perceived as being closest to the Lord and greater than their fellow brothers.

The profound conclusion is that Christ did not wrestle with any mental gymnastics. He simply taught them, then challenged them on who was the greatest by testing which one could prove they loved Him the most. He challenged them to see who was willing to wash the lowliest of dirty feet in pure servitude. Christ wanted to know who was courageous to stand by Him when they were challenged as a known follower of His. The disciples resolved their own problems within themselves to understand that they were all equal in the eyes of Christ and God. They could only be equal if they would do what He did, which was for the least of them. They would also need to remain focused on saving the lost and ministering others into redemption with Christ, to whom all would kneel in exhortation and reverence.

Lastly, not one, no, not even one of disciples could pay the price or was worthy to secure salvation and redemption of the world. That is what Christ was born for. There was one disciple, however, who Christ had purposed a greater calling on His life for an explicit great work, where He would put His mother Mary into the trust and home of the disciple John. His half-brother James and John were important in the nurturing of His mother. No doubt they would fill the void in her heart and emptiness in her home after losing her beloved son. His death was not for waste, for His name amongst the people became known as being powerful in miracles and speaking the parables of God's truths, knowledge and salvation unto grace and heaven bound after death with Him.

"When Jesus saw his mother there, and the disciple whom he loved standing nearby, he said to her, "Woman, here is your son,"
and to the disciple, "Here is your mother." From that time on,
this disciple took her into his home." (John 19: 26-27)

ANTIDOTE 14 |
HONOR YOUR MOTHER
AND FATHER

"A son is the reflection of his father in the sun, and the daughter is the reflection of her mother in the mirror." Erogies Grigley Jr.

Why do you find it so hard to honor your mother and father? Did they not bear your childhood burdens and love you unconditionally? Relationships can be hard, but the work is well worth the joys and pleasures of family and friends. There must be an abiding and kindred spirit that helps parents and children to be on one accord. The realization must be that a child can never exceed their parents, as they are both patriarch and matriarch, head of the family and covers them with unconditional love. Should you honor your parents all of their days, as this is pleasing unto the Lord? *"Honor your father and your mother, so that you may live long in the land the Lord your God is giving you." (Exodus 20:12)*

A mother and father must demonstrate and teach the love and honor of Jesus Christ. Their love of each other is demonstrated through kind interactions, personal sacrifices, total respect, honor and uncompromised trust and humility – in words and actions. This discipline and loving humble lifestyle will propel a prosperous, long and joyous respectful life in the family, along their paths in *the art of living well*, for and with the Creator and the Source. A son will not be a ruin to his father and a daughter will not be a disgrace to her mother, if love and honor is the absolute desire of both the parents and the child.

Where there is love, dignity is the golden standard and honor with virtues and character are the foundations upon which one can stand, as is the Word of the Lord. You must embrace the innocence of a child in their love and honor towards their parents. This attitude is under subrogation and in the Spirit of the Lord, to receive the teaching that exceeds that of the parents. The teachings include parents not provoking their children but to love, raise, teach and protect them, which are from the book of Proverbs and the Holy Spirit. The profound teachings are not of a parent's carnal nature, but of the love and compassion of the Source, and God Himself. God sent the parents beforehand as children, to become adults, in order to understand what a child goes through. If you are willing to do the Source's Will, you will not only know of the foundations of Christ's teachings, but you will experience the righteousness and unconditional love of the rich blessings from the Lord and hold them dear in your heart. Even as adults, children should honor their parents and parents should not provoke their children. *"Fathers, do not exasperate your children; instead, bring them up in the training and instruction of the Lord." (Ephesians 6:4)*

Children are children and as a child, will do childish things. It is in a child's young nature to be contrary and in some cases, necessary in their discovery towards growing up. But, once you reached adulthood, you put childish ways aside and walk in the maturity of manhood and womanhood, honorably. This does not mean that once you become a man or woman and live in your own home, you have to obey your parents in all things instructed. Rather, regardless of your age, you must always honor your parents, as long as they both shall live. As mature adults, particularly married, you can honor your parents, while not always doing exactly what they want. For you and your spouse must live together, get along and prosper as one and as a family in your own home. The teeth and tongue live together in a very tight home, and sometimes fall out with one another. But, daily, they learn to live together in harmony and discipline. As a full fledge and mature adult, you do not have to always obey your parents' desires, but you must honor and respect them as your parents with dignity and grace, resting in humility, whether you live in their home or in your own house. Honor is required! *"Honor your father and your mother, so that you may live long in the land the LORD your God is giving you." (Exodus 20:12)*

Never take liberty to boast from within yourself and in your teaching for your own glory. This would be unrighteous for you to deny the righteousness of the Source and Creator, who are Lord and God, in which there is no unrighteousness or self-seeking. Instead, seek to glorify the Source and the Creator without accolades to edify your ego. When you sincerely seek the Lord's mind and strive to be obedient unto the Lord, you are empowered to share the Lord's teachings and observances to the whole home. Allow the peace of Christ to rule your heart, mind, soul and spirit to keep the flesh in subjection against worldly and unrighteous desires. Be on one accord and one body for the whole house to serve the Lord and be thankful. There should be an infilling of the Word of the Lord to richly dwell within you, spoken gently with His wisdom in all aspects of teaching and even admonishing and challenging one another. Have joys and songs of worship, praise and thanksgiving in your heart unto the Lord, grateful in consistently teaching them to your family and friends. *"Tell it to your children, and let your children tell it to their children, and their children to the next generation." (Joel 1:3)* Know and embrace that whatever is done in both word and works must be done in the name of the Source our Lord. In doing so, give heartfelt and spiritual truth of thanks through Jesus Christ, unto His Father, God the Creator.

As parents on one accord, your young children will sit on your laps with kindled joy. However, if your children mature without honor and reverence for matriarch and patriarch, they will bring rebellion to the Lord's

Word. These parents' days will be filled with tears and years of pain. When children mature, the hope is they would bring a smile to their parent's faces. Their prayers are for the Source to keep them humble, courageous and loving. Towards the path's end, parents will wax and grow old, eyes will go dim, and backs will bend from days of pain and years of toil. They will yearn for destiny to come at midnight or morning dawn. It matters not the hour; for the appointed time shall come where each person will account for demonstrated acts and validated good works related to belief in the Source. This will be accompanied by confessions of repentance and forgiveness, living in His righteousness, faith and justification. There should be a falling in love with the Son Jesus Christ that expresses obedience and humility to your father and mother.

There are children who bring smiles and create joyful hopes in your tomorrows. Each child has a different spirit of excellence and gratefulness. However, all have received the same level of love, values, morals and principles which to live by. Yet, as some children get older, they become a child that cries on your heart. An ole' saying is "Today, the child sits on your lap and brings laughter; tomorrow, they will grow up and sit on your heart and bring you tears". It does not matter what home one grows up in, the value of appreciation is deeply rooted in the affectionate love and demonstrated admiration in the home. The love for Christ, love for parents, love for grandparents, love for family and love for neighbors and friends create a healthy community.

Children grounded in scriptural principles which are taught daily and tough love in the home cannot be matched or a value placed on. Do not give children too much, because they will become enabled to be contrary, spoiled and have false expectations as they get older. Their lives should not be surrounded with materialism; rather shrouded in humility, thanksgiving, hard work, respect and trust. Teach them to give to the least and less fortunate children and seniors, as lessons of humility and service in life. These tenants and the strictness of assuring they are carried out builds, shapes and molds the child into mature and justified manhood and womanhood. Giving parents wonderful moments and memories, today and tomorrow, in Christ. *"He must manage his own family well and see that his children obey him, and he must do so in a manner worthy of full respect." (1 Timothy 3:4)*

Finally, parents' twilight years will arrive, and they will be filled with the Spirit of the Lord Jesus Christ and belief in the Creator's Sovereignty and Omnipotence, in word, spirit, truth and glory. Be careful your behavior does not send parents to tarry in the hot sun and experience dark lonely nights. Avoid being disobedient and troublesome acts, which will follow your parents to the cemetery with thoughts of what life could have been. Friends, before the hour is too late for you or your parents, my pleas are for you to love, obey, honor and enjoy your parents. For the day will come where your laughter will change to tears, as your child gets older and parents fade away.

Parents adore your children in agape and tough love, to grow in maturity and reverence for the Lord, for this is the Will of the Source and Messiah. Remember, love covers a multitude of sins and failures, and agape love never fails. Therefore, love and honor your parents, all their days, that your children will reciprocate these same tenants to you. Remember what you were when you were children and the expectations of your parents towards you and your obedience.

"Brothers and sisters, think of what you were when you were called. Not many of you were wise by human standards; not many were influential; not many were of noble birth. But God chose the foolish things of the world to shame the wise; God chose the weak things of the world to shame the strong...Let the one who boasts boast in the Lord" (1 Corinthians 1:26-31)

ANTIDOTE 15 |
KNOW YOUR CAPACITY

"If one understands and subdues their desires and emotions, specifically those things which belong to or concerns another person, the less misunderstandings will arise." Erogies Grigley Jr.

Do you know who you are in principle and the strength of your capacity, in order to live bountifully and overcome your perceived spiraling vortex life? Everyone goes through the filtering process of life's negative and positive experiences. Many people learn to understand and grow from their desires versus being discipline as a disciple which plays a large part in one's living. If you reduce your earthly and worldly desires, the less of a desire will stir inside your mind and heart for fleeting satisfactions. *"With many similar parables Jesus spoke the word to them, as much as they could understand." (Mark 4:33)*

When you become learnt in the way of the warrior spirit to be discipline in all things, the lesser the desires to acquire greater control. You will develop your inner and physical strengths to accomplish great feats by the Lord's favor. Each person is created differently for the singular purpose of the Creator's Will on earth and is born with different capacities to give and to receive. Yet, each person can freely give and receive as desired. Everyone is born for a purpose and must discover their cause in life from the Source. He knows you well and only desires that you do well in life, while carrying out His Will. *"In the beginning was the Word, and the Word was with God, and the Word was God. He was with God in the beginning. Through him all things were made; without him nothing was made that has been made. In him was life, and that life was the light of all mankind. The light shines in the darkness, and the darkness has not overcome it." (1 John 1:1-5)*

If fleshly desires grow stronger, so too will the control to use your assets to gain the identified desires of opportunities – usually emotional, physical and material. If you understand and subdue your desires, specifically those things which belong to another person, the less misunderstandings will arise, and you will not find fault with the other. The cycle of mental desires become fleshly, repeated and lead you down a destructive path. For some, this will involve pain, ruin and heartbreak; for others, loss of a loved one or suicide. Our societies have become engulfed in capitalism and creation of false desires as norms in life. People prey on giving satisfaction from false things not needed, by advertising and promoting increasing happiness through bad spending and purchasing – where you do not value your dollars. This cycle not only gets repeated, but it is transferred from parents to their children. Thus, the capitalistic appeal to be a part of capitalism in society through material ownership continues, without any end in sight.

There is a myth, as old as religion, philosophies and doctrines of modern civilization, that all men and women are created equal. Everyone is not equal, on earth, in humanity or spirituality in creation. Yes, God created everyone, but He gave everyone free wills and free minds, not the same wills and not the same minds, to exercise intellectually and physically. The Creator did not create everyone equal with no respecter of persons. The Source gives no living being of having the same physical and mental capacity, same makeup, same gifts, same talents or same opportunities. You must come into a full knowledge and understanding that God is no respecter of persons. Neither is He concerned about any person's will, unless their will is in His Will! Each person is created differently for the singular purpose of the Creator's Will and born with a different capacity to give and to receive, to achieve and to fail. If you embrace the allegory that balloons come in different sizes and colors, one can vividly use wisdom with understanding to conclude not one person is created equal in this world.

We must embrace how small we are individually, and how positive impacting we are collectively in God. The Scripture confirms that each individual can perform different services through differing gifts. *"Therefore, I want you to know that no one who is speaking by the Spirit of God says, "Jesus be cursed," and no one can say, "Jesus is Lord," except by the Holy Spirit. There are different kinds of gifts…, Now to each one the manifestation of the Spirit is given for the common good, to another faith by the same Spirit… All these are the work of one and the same Spirit, and he distributes them to each one, just as he determines." (1 Corinthians 12:3-11)*

As a young boy, during summer heat waves in the Deep South of Midway, Florida, my youthful siblings, friends and I would find fortune in water balloon fights. Each would purchase a pack of different-sized balloons to fit intended strategy. The sizes ranged from small balloons that fit into one hand after being blown up and filled with water and medium balloons that were either wider or longer and exceeded the size of one's hand when filled with air and water. The large balloons took longer to fill with air and water and required both hands.

The balloon fights were harmless and created a great deal of fun and laughter as we filled our balloons with water and stacked them as artillery rounds to be launched at opponents. In this discovery, I learned that small balloons that held a pint of air expanded to two pints of water. A medium-sized balloon could hold a quart of air and expand. A large balloon could hold a half gallon of air and expand to almost one gallon of water. In handling different-sized balloons filled with different amounts of water, the difficulty to throw with precision was altered tremendously.

The pint-sized balloon filled with water could be handled like a baseball and thrown with great accuracy in short and long distances. The medium-sized balloon could be handled with a controlled degree of difficulty liken to throwing a football with a reduced level of distance and accuracy. The gallon-sized balloon of water was handled clumsily like a basketball or big bag of Jell-O with very short-range distances, only to come within arm's reach of an opponent, and even then, with flawed accuracy. In comparing a person's capacity to a balloon capacity, you will discover that balloons can expand in size when filled with water. We must be filled with faith and the Holy Spirit to enjoy an abundant life, regardless of our differences, pedigrees, and expectations. *"But even if I am being poured out like a drink offering on the sacrifice and service coming from your faith, I am glad and rejoice with all of you. So you too should be glad and rejoice with me." (Philippians 2:17-18)*

People have minds and spirits that can be expanded in size, when filled with the Sources' Spirit – in wisdom, knowledge, understanding and anointing – living water. I have matured and observed in the natural and spirit realm that the Lord can take average pint-sized people who are gallon size in capacity, cognitively and physically and have them accomplish great feats. God is able to improve your common sense and spiritually expand to twice or one hundred times that of your expectations. The increase is in mind, physical and spiritual makeup. In using gallons to demonstrate the capacity of people not being created equal, the discovery is that all people have a base and optimum expansion to exercise giving and receiving. It is the Living Water that gives you increase in knowledge, wisdom and understanding, that can take an unlearnt person and transformed them into the wise and sought-after leader.

In example, a one-gallon size person or large balloon is able to reach an optimum expansion of two gallons when the balloons are filled with water – cognitively, physically, common sense and spiritually without an anointing. Likewise, a five or ten-gallon capacity person or balloon cannot expand to reach optimums of ten and twenty-gallon capacities when filled with water – cognitively, common sense and spiritually without an anointing. A time will come when and where you give freely but are limited to give out of and at your optimum capacity. You are very beneficial to the people who are less in capacity to you. In the same way, when you receive, you are not limited to receive at your optimum mental capacity, but beneficial to people in your spiritual capacity. When a ten-gallon balloon sized person attempts to pour into a two-gallon balloon sized person, the maximum knowledge, wisdom, and spiritual discernment they are able to take on is four gallons in the natural realm.

Any amount of knowledge, wisdom and spiritual input greater than four-gallons, poured into four-gallon size people will likely spill out to the ground. The same is inverse, in that if a five-gallon person attempts to pour into a ten-gallon person, very little will be gained as the optimum knowledge, wisdom and spiritual input from the five-gallon sized balloon person. We must realize that the ten-gallon person's base, as they are naturally, are able to expand to twenty gallons without resistance or having pre-conceived and learnt behaviors that limit their acceptance of such expansion. In essence, this ten-gallon balloon sized person actually requires someone with equal or higher capacity to pour into them.

In the spiritual and physical realm, it is simplistic to challenge the US Declaration of Independence that says, "We hold these truths to be self-evident, that {all men are created equal}, that they are endowed by their Creator with certain unalienable Rights, that among these are Life, Liberty and the pursuit of Happiness." This is a splendid and magnificent capture of potent and calibrated perfected English, yet without merit and truth to some as created equal in the rights and respect as full fledge American citizens. *Do not show partiality in judging; hear both small and the great alike. Do not be afraid of anyone, for judgment belongs to God. Bring me any case too hard for you, and I will hear it. And at that time, I told you every-thing you were to do." (Deuteronomy 1:17-18)*

Thereby, these words in active voice are contrary and view ethnicities and women as less than equal, and rarely can you fulfill this equality. The grace of God creates faith towards opportunities to open doors along the journey towards your destiny. In the same way, a time will come, when people will give and receive freely, not limited to just giving at your base capacity. *"You call yourselves citizens of the holy city and claim to rely on the God of Israel – but not in truth or righteousness – the Lord Almighty is his name." (Isaiah 48:2)*

Do not become frustrated or feel inferior or superior to a higher or lesser capacity person; rather meet them where they are, as they are. Make it known that in accepting Christ, with obedience and great faith all things are possible, and all are equal in His eyes. In the twinkling of an eye, through your good works, perseverance and pursuits of excellence, God can change your life immensely, for the better. Where you are, or where you were, is not the end of your journey or accomplishments. Appreciate what you have. Give thanks for where you are but know that you can do more and achieve better with the Source and Creator. If you feel uncomfortable and do not like where you are and what you have accomplished, then rise and change your status, even the environment if necessary. You can achieve that which you set your heart, mind, spirit, soul and strength to. The poten-tial is endless with these unique and assured blends of discipline efforts, meticulous planning and committed pursuits. *"Then Peter began to speak: 'I now realize how true it is that God does not show favoritism but accepts from every nation the one who fears him and does what is right.'" (Acts 10:34-35)*

With differing purposes and differing gifts, you can have what is for you, in God's Will by doing what is right! More favorably, you can uplift and give hope to others just with a good word. Persons who share similar lifestyles and perspectives are more likely to have more in common and can relate. Shared personalities will create a climate more effective and favorable for fostering growth, as well as achieving higher performance and leading to freely making positive life changes. *"You are the salt of the earth. But if the salt loses its saltiness, how can it be made salty again? It is no longer good for anything…You are the light of the world. A town built on a hill cannot be hidden." (Matthew 5:13-14)*

This becomes a win-win, as each person in their respective capacities pour into others of less and equal capacities to help make them better. You must feel, know, see and speak "I am" through their spiritual DNA and initiate movement within their Genetic Code, which is connected to the Vine, the Source. Through the Source, you possess the ability to embrace equality of spiritual enlightenment and in the truths to live fully. Choose to freely give, serve, love and forgive in your quest to bear divine fruits for a bountiful harvest. Spiritual enlightenment will always prevail, as God dwells in the midst of the disciplined, faithful and good-hearted person, who is in the center of His perfect Will and where there are no boundaries or limitations in righteousness and good.

"But since you excel in everything – in faith, in speech, in knowledge, in complete earnestness and in the love we have kindled in you – see that you also excel in this grace of giving. I am not commanding you, but I want to test the sincerity of your love by comparing it with the earnestness of others. For you know the grace of our Lord Jesus Christ, that though he was rich, yet for your sake he became poor, so that you through his poverty might become rich." (2 Corinthians 8:7-9)

ANTIDOTE 16 |
WRESTLING WITH GOD'S WILL

"Wrestle with God for His Will on your life, in reminding
Him of His promises and holding on by faith, grace and hope
for the due season, due to you." Erogies Grigley Jr.

Can you test your will against God's Will, to change your life and purpose? You were born with a free will spirit to choose between good and evil, principles and corruption, morality and dishonor. There must be a pricking of the heart and vexing of the spirit, to embrace change and be humbled to do the Will of the higher authority, than to reside in the lowliness of selfishness. *"He is always wrestling in prayer for you, that you may stand firm in all the will of God, mature and fully assured." (Colossians 4:12)*

A test of wills occurs each day between people, corporations, Mother Nature, the universe and cosmos, the church and even the world for the purpose of keeping life balanced as a part of Creation. Where would I be if I had not believed I would see the Lord's favor? God's Will is Sovereign and pure, while your will is selfish and conceited.

Paul, an apostle of Christ Jesus, by the Will of God, gave the Gospel to God's holy people and those who were not exposed to the Word, with a focus on faithfulness and obedience. *"Grace and peace to you from God our Father and the Lord Jesus Christ. Praise be to the God and Father of our Lord Jesus Christ, who has blessed us in the heavenly realms with every spiritual blessing in*

Christ. For he chose us in Him before the creation of the world to be holy and blameless in his sight. In love He predestined us for adoption to sonship through Jesus Christ, in accordance with His pleasure and will – to the praise of His glorious grace, which He has freely given us in the One He loves." (Ephesians 1:2-6)

Never limit or stop your faith in action. Be positive and say, "God I won't let go until you bless me!" God and the Lord created man and woman for His purpose, companionship and to have dominion authority over all of earth and creations therein. God intentionally provided humankind the free will spirit to make free choices in life. The belief was people with His spirit in them would always align their ethical and moral compass in the natural and spiritual orders. *"So Jacob was left alone, and a man wrestled with him till daybreak. When the man saw that he could not overpower him, he touched the socket of Jacob's hip so that his hip was wrenched as he wrestled with the man. Then the man said, 'Let me go, for it is daybreak.' But Jacob replied, 'I will not let you go unless you bless me...' Then the man said, 'Your name will no longer be Jacob, but Israel, because you have struggled with God and with humans and have overcome... Then he blessed him there.' So Jacob called the place Peniel, saying, 'It is because I saw God face to face, and yet my life was spared.'" (Genesis 32:24-30)*

The greatest tests are belief, trust, obedience, discipline, faith, perseverance and love in and of God. God wants you to accept the Messiah as your Lord, Him as your Father and live in obedience to His Word. If you share in these tenants and precepts, you are encouraged to wrestle with God for His Will on your life. For your relationship is founded on better promises through Christ, by faith, grace and hope for the seasons due to you. It is your season. Pursue and walk in the sunlight and the rain. You should be encouraged to wrestle with God like Jacob, in spirituality, prayer and faith to walk into your new destiny, new increase, new breakthroughs for health, finances, home, career, your children and calling. You are to be whole as victors and not victims, favored and not failures, gifted and not grieved, prosperous and not psychotic. *"I remain confident of this: I will see the goodness of the LORD in the land of the living. Wait for the LORD; be strong and take heart and wait for the LORD." (Psalm 27:13-14)*

State your declaration and reach out to the Lord in your obedience and great faith. Draw the power from Emmanuel's veins of living waters to help you be victorious. It is your expectancy for Jesus to bless you, as are His promises to stop and make you and your needs His priorities. Keep convincing yourself in hope and faith with the Lord to move according to the Scriptures with great 'now' faith, a contrite spirit and broken heart. God must move to do what He has written, *"I will bless you and never abandon you!" (Psalm 37:28)* He will bless you in your belief, faith and obedience, to the Son and Father, in your living and journey. He loves you unconditionally as the Sovereign God that He is. You are His and He is yours, through Jesus Christ, for ever and ever. *"Then my head will be exalted above the enemies who surround me…; Hear my voice when I call, LORD; be merciful to me and answer me. My heart says of you, 'Seek his face!' Your face, LORD, I will seek. Do not hide your face from me, do not turn your servant away in anger; you have been my helper. Do not reject me or forsake me, God my Savior." (Psalm 27:6-9)*

You can take solace in wrestling with God in prayer and conversation unceasingly until God moves with a suddenness and supernaturally. Let your faith lead you into being steadfast for His promises to be fulfilled for you. Now, the brook the Lord took you to has dried up and His loving actions are required to deliver you. Before Jesus went to suffer, He spent hours in the late night and midnight hours praying to His Father. He wanted God to have mercy and show compassion upon Him as the only begotten Son and perhaps not have to experience the horrific suffering and agony of death before Him. It is the belief that Christ did not fear dying; rather, He dreaded being separated from God in His deepest despair and expectant pains to come. As the Son, even He wanted His Will answered, and He wanted to be delivered from this seemingly terrible task befallen upon Himself. Even though Christ asked God three times to take the bitter cup away, God did not answer Him. Therefore, Jesus said, *"Abba, Father,"* he said, *"everything is possible for you. Take this cup from me. Yet not what I will, but what you will." (Mark 14:36)*

It can never be about your will, nor that of your sinful nature. Everything in life must be about God's Will and Christ's Sovereign guidance, in the center of God's Will. Therein, in this place of solace and majesty, shall we find truth, meaning and fulfillment in Christ and *the art of living well.*

"To you, LORD, I call; you are my Rock, do not turn a deaf ear to me. For if you remain silent, I will be like those who go down to the pit. Hear my cry for mercy as I call to you for help, as I lift up my hands toward your Most Holy Place." (Psalm 28:1-2)

ANTIDOTE 17 |
VALUE EVERY DOLLAR

"When money is spent, it becomes buried, sunk, burned and destroyed.
It is gone from your hands forever." Erogies Grigley Jr.

Can you make dollars back, which were spent or given away? Money comes and money goes, but only the wise and prudent understand it is not so much the amount you make; rather, it is the amount you save and invest that determines if your needs will be met for a good future. Once a dollar is spent, you cannot get it back or make the dollar back. When something is buried, sunk, burned, or destroyed, it is gone forever; so is money once spent. *"Who will judge its quality as good or bad. Whatever value the priest then sets, that is what it will be." (Leviticus 27:12)*

You must leave the state of denial in understanding money, for stewardship of money is the answer to all things. When you exchange money for goods or services, you cannot get those dollars back; they are gone forever into the new hands of capitalism and the deceiver. Although you cannot get the specific dollar back, you can be wise and prudent, and make a different dollar, which you can choose not to spend. However, your future is grossly affected, as the potential power for this dollar to create your liberties, joys, peace of mind and higher quality of life is also lost with its demise. God wants you to work and enjoy the work of your hands, mind, talents and gifts, as well the fruits of your labor. For in working, with a sense of purpose and dignity, you find excellence in how you live and the source to living abundantly. *"For we are God's handiwork, created in Christ Jesus to do good works, which God prepared in advance for us to do." (Ephesians 2:10)*

You must not conform to the pressures, patterns and proclivities of this capitalist and carnal world; rather, be diligent in consistently and constantly transforming yourself for mining new treasures in spirit and discovery of heart, talents and gifts. To reinvent your foresight is to increase the pliability of your heart and renewing of your mind – to believe in the value of money, which is wise. Do not develop and embrace the love of money, which is evil and destructive to oneself and family, generationally. You must die daily to the woes and distractions of the world that demand spending and releasing your lifetime of earning millions of dollars. *"Wealth lost through some misfortune, so that when they have children there is nothing left for them to inherit..." (Ecclesiastes 5:14)*

The evil one lives and moves upon the earth to give you a false converted means of power, greed and control in your decision-making to spend and live from paycheck to paycheck. When you receive pay for performance, does your chin ride high in pride? When you make God first, you seek Him and His righteousness in all things first. The earth's offering becomes the Lord's heavenly provision for you to have abundance in life. Your spiritual growth and loving personal relationship with Jesus Christ the Son and Source, and God the Creator, assure you of the Mediator's promise to anoint your life for longevity and prosperity. In acknowledging the Source, His power and authority endows His beloved ones' senses and monetary provisions to be multiplied. Money is needed to answer all things on earth – in abounding or abashing. *"A feast is made for laughter, wine makes life merry, and money is the answer for everything." (Ecclesiastes 10:19)*

Your gifting and covenant fellowship with the Lord should be steadfast to build trust and to test God's Will for your dollars, for your family and life. You must become a wise steward, full of knowledge and understand monetary stewardship to build financial ownership and growth. As a disciple, friend and steward of God, you are prudent without concern for rendering to Caesar and to man only what is theirs. You render to God what is the Lords', for God owns all and the Lord's will is good, perfect and powerful with purpose for His glory. Remember that money is important and useful in all things on earth, and for the upbuilding of God's Kingdom. Treasure money, but never let money treasure you or guide you. Be led by the Spirit of God and the wonderful utterance of the inner-being by the Holy Spirit. You should always give bountifully unto the Lord and ask His guidance for all monies He blesses you with.

You are encouraged to develop a lifestyle of obedience and will power to build a financial and personal value scorecard of your resources. If you plan wisely with your time, gifts, talents and voice, you will experience an abundant living along the path's journey with the Lord, in *the art of living well*. In changing your perspectives, you will subconsciously implement enlightenment. This will lead to a brighter path which never reaches to the poor level of being irresponsible and unaccountable. Refrain from being foolish in your ways, failing to mature. Put childish behavior away and act like a rationale adult with ownership for tomorrow. *"I have seen a grievous evil under the sun: wealth hoarded to the harm of the owners."* *(Ecclesiastes 5:13)*

No man or woman can change the Father's Will and Son's purpose established for you. You are the one called by Him, as His own and He always take great joy in being your Mediator. Not only this, but Jesus is your Intercessor and navigator during your journey of life, along the path where His divine Will is made known and manifested for His purpose and the Father's glory through you, His spiritual agent.

A dollar has great value only on earth. It cannot travel through time and space to enter heaven. The dollar is worldly, man-made, and the love of the dollar is evil in actions on earth and in the eyes of the Source and

Creator. If you value monetary potential as added value for life, through God's blessings and your stewardship, He will multiply your dollars. With a certain level of risk, if you spend a portion of your dollars to purchase assets, can the dollars be made back? No. Only new dollars that are not spent can be made to replace the ones spent. The spent dollars are lost forever.

Though paper currency has lesser value than silver and gold, the dollar's capacity is embraced to provide for your present needs, quality of life and greater opportunities. But greater than these, God favors the just and righteous and pours blessings out of the windows of heaven as spiritual prosperity that is manifested as currency. Your dollars should be used for the upbuilding of His Kingdom and serve His tables which includes at minimum, the church and providing for widows, orphans, the sick and the poor. *"This is what the LORD Almighty said: 'Administer true justice; show mercy and compassion to one another. Do not oppress the widow or the fatherless, the foreigner or the poor. Do not plot evil against each other.'" (Zechariah 7:9-10)*

The Lord's desire is for all that are called by His name to know peace, joy and bountiful fruits with celebrations and feasts, by which the dollar surely can bring to your home. The dollar is cash, and as such, the dollar must be viewed and embraced figuratively and literally as king, as credit must be viewed and hugged figuratively and literally as queen. Together, when cash and credit, king and queen, are on one accord in submission to the Lord for the allocation of the dollar, their formidable powers are too great to be challenged or swindled by the craftiness of the evil and destructive ones. Imperative is the understanding that the evil ones are full of greed and destruction, with paramount aim to make you a worldly human of weaker flesh and carnal mind, with a shallow spirit to be known simply as an ignorant consumer and spender – squanderers. *"Trouble pursues the sinner, but the righteous are rewarded with good things. A good person leaves an inheritance for their children's children, but a sinner's wealth is stored up for the righteous." (Proverbs 13:21-22)*

You must be acute in spiritual awareness of this jealous one, who is a master of cunning thoughts to offer you the great deals, sales and promotions of allure and false beliefs of achieving a great bargain. The evil one of capitalism is at envy with God and thrives to steal every dollar, even your soul. If you are thriving in the world, with worldly lifestyles, you are at enmity with God. Regardless of being earned from legal and respectable laboring, over months and years, the evil one wants it all. In an instance, the dollars are spent. The dollars and the value are no more, for you have acquired vain material possessions and fleeting instant gratification, along with loss value of the items purchased. When you spend money acquiring a bunch of materialistic things over time, this spending behavior results in valuable dollars being gone forever. This will leave you worst emotionally and physically, as your monies and treasures are given away, sunk, buried, consumed and burned, which you cannot get back. *"Do not give dogs what is sacred; do not throw your pearls to pigs. If you do, they may trample them under their feet, and turn and tear you to pieces." (Matthew 7:6)*

Though of lesser value than silver and gold, the dollar's capacity is embraced to provide for your present needs, quality of life, greater opportunities, a future and leaving an inheritance.

Greater than these, God favors you and pours out of the windows of heaven spiritual prosperity that is manifested as currency. Know well, that it is only the Lord who can give increase, not man, machine or your will. Favor and increase, under grace, must be His Will! Never have a craving or love for money, for this attitude and behavior will cause you and your dollars to be sifted into separate particles and tossed into the wind for others to take and steal. "For the love of money is a root of all kinds of evil. Some people, eager for money, have wandered from the faith and pierced themselves with many griefs." (1 Timothy 6:10) You must embrace wisdom and get understanding in dealing with money, for your attempt to protect wisdom is like you valiantly trying to protect money. The advantage of getting knowledge, wisdom and understanding money and all things, is that only wisdom will preserve your life, whether you have or do not have wealth.

Important in this Antidote is reminding you that you can have living waters from heaven and thirst no more for wealth. You are to have good work ethics and apply yourself to exhorting the Lord in your ways and thoughts that are of God's Will. He will enable you to purchase the needs for your life, through the Source. He will even send people bearing gifts to your bosom, paying for your groceries in line, giving you envelopes filled with money and making deposits to your bank account. Look at storing up treasures in your heart first for heaven, then for the poor and needy, downtrodden, lowly and sick. Now, you can store up monetary treasures for your future with banks and investments, expecting the Lord to bless and multiply what He has given you. The key is to not be selfish and con-ceited. Do not harbor money and things. Do not be filled with greed and an incorruptible spirit to gain immorally at the defeat and destruction of others. *"Do not store up for yourselves treasures on earth...; But store up for yourselves treasures in heaven, where moths and vermin do not destroy...; For where your treasure is, there your heart will be also." (Matthew 6:19-21)*

The ways of the Lord are to bless those that live righteously, those who keep His word, and those who chase after His heart. Serve the Lord with gladness and enter into His gates with thanksgiving in your spirit, heart and mind. And, enter into His court with gratefulness, praise and testimony on your lips, joy in your soul, of how wonderful and awesome God is and majestic and miraculous is Jesus Christ!

The Dollar Allocation Model accounts for each quarter and requires the quarters to be allocated as dollars before they arrive at your bank account or are spent. This table helps to prevent you from spending unwisely and from being wasteful. You must establish a budget for managing your earned income, which also helps you in investing and contributes to producing intellectual and passive income. Use the Dollar Allocation Model below and stay within the percentages. Be sure to converse with your Circle of Expert Advisors. You who live a noble and successful life outperform those in lesser capacity for a brighter tomorrow and wealthier future. *"Discretion will protect you, and understanding will guard you." (Proverbs 2:11)*

The Dollar Allocation Model should be adhered to with the seriousness of frugalness, sacrifice and discipline. The model helps you to live within your means. Also, to consider living beneath your means to achieve financial independence and wealth building in a more rapid rate of returns. Invest much earlier in life to focus on your purpose and fulfilling the passion of your love for your *art of living.* You can assure financial freedom by investing 20% of your paycheck between ages 25 to 60. You can realize financial freedom over time by investing monies into an index fund that provides a modest 10%-15% return, using the Rule of 72. If you embrace this philosophy, your future income yield will be built over time through income averaging where you have capital and dividend accumulation to achieve a million dollars.

There can be great joys in having money, even to know great peace. But, living with more always begets others to want more of what you have. Money is not the root of evil; rather, Scripture records that it is the love of money that causes destruction. It is critically important not to become emotional in your spending with or without money. Learn to be content in your disciplined way of life. This gives way to building more financial freedom and independence, while respecting and valuing what you have and finding joy in what you have built, through Christ. *"Keep your lives free from the love of money and be content with what you have, because God has said, 'Never will I leave you; never will I forsake you." (Hebrews 13:5)*

The Dollar Allocation chart on page 118 is significant in being disciplined in your giving, saving, investing and helping – in this order. Know your boundaries, and pray for financial wisdom, knowledge and understanding. Money has its purpose and can help supply all of your earthly needs. Everyone needs money, even the church, in order to survive and be in the purpose of God, for His Will and in providing provisions for the journey of life. Use the chart and live within it, that your days may be long and prosperous, every day.

A sure way to achieve wealth and financial independence is to change your attitude and principles toward money. Focus on finding an asset as an entrepreneur, such as real estate and an index fund to pay for an expense that you would like to purchase. The asset could be buying and selling real estate, index funds, antique cars or as a consultant or speaker. With real estate, you could purchase a property for passive income from rents; or, buy and sell the property asset to make a sizeable profit towards your other purchases. The simplicity of the complex is to repeat this principle dozens of times to build passive, intellectual and entrepreneur income.

"On the first day of every week, each one of you should set aside a sum of money in keeping with your income, saving it up, so that when I come no collections will have to be made." (1 Corinthians 16:2)

Dollar Allocation Model

DOLLAR ALLOCATION BY AREA	PERCENTAGES
Church, Charities, Philanthropy	10
Retirement: 401K, ROTH, TSP	10
Investments: M-Funds, Stocks, Real Estate	20
Emergency Savings	10
Personal: Clothing	3
Home Ownership	20
Food & Restaurants	3
Bills: Utilities, Furnishings, Credit	2
Vacation & Travel	4
Insurance: Medical, Dental, Vision	4
Life Insurance, Annuities	2
Auto Loan	4
Education	4
Transportation, Gas	2
Entertainment	2
Total	100

ANTIDOTE 18 |
CREATE A CIRCLE OF EXPERTS AND ADVISORS

"You must have a Circle of Expert Advisors to provide you with the necessary knowledge, wisdom and understanding of all aspects of life for the journey you embark on." Erogies Grigley Jr.

Are you lacking in confidence because you are fearful of what others think of you? Are you lacking in wisdom and understanding? This thinking brings on suffering and low self-esteem, in that you have not, because you seek not and ask not. Lack of confidence is not knowing who you are and not having a circle of friends who hold you accountable and lend a hand to see that you are successful. Do you oppose to having a circle of accountable friends and advisors in your life? Do you acquiesce from being responsible and accountable? This is dangerous to your character and promotes selfish behaviors and regretful actions. *"One who has unreliable friends soon comes to ruin, but there is a friend who sticks closer than a brother." (Proverbs 18:24)*

When different opportunities, challenges and decision-making conditions rise to the occasion, you must be able to seek counsel and expert advice. You must surround your life with a Circle of Experts & Advisors who operate successfully and higher levels than you are. Conversing with your Circle of Experts & Advisors who live a noble and successful life, outperforming you in capacity and higher levels will significantly contribute to ethical and viable decisions for a brighter tomorrow. At minimum, the focus should include a healthier life, balanced family, assets ownership, wealth and leaving an inheritance for a joyous future. *"For lack of guidance a nation falls, but victory is won through many advisers." (Proverbs 11:14)*

The Circle of Experts & Advisors Model on page 123 should be a part of your life, so you can live a modest and respectful life full of high principles. The Circle of Expert & Advisors should be combined of at least the advisors, mentors and coaches in the chart to prevent mistakes, long nights and catastrophes. The experts and advisors will help you increase the likelihood of experiencing joy, financial well-being, sound decisions, and restful in *the art of living.*

Once you establish your budget using the Dollar Allocation Model and address your financial concerns and earned income with the Circle of Advisors & Experts, then you can tell your quarters where to go based on facts and the best advice. Surround yourself with true believers in Christ and let their favor become your blessings and successes in good and tough times. *"But let all who take refuge in you be glad; let them ever sing for joy. Spread your protection over them, that those who love your name may rejoice in you. Surely, LORD, you bless the righteous; you surround them with your favor as with a shield." (Psalm 5:11-12)*

Not only can you live within your means, but you can also live beneath your means, which allows you to save and invest more. Also, this attitude and lifestyle will help you to live and capture wonderful and breathtaking memories for a lifetime. You own the decision for your monies, as no one can tell you what to do, nor should you let anyone tell you what to do. You own the decision for your actions!

Because you have told your quarters where to go to take care of you, you can live the way you want to in the present and in the future. If you are wise and consistent in living a modest lifestyle and invest over time, you will be able retire between ages 40-50, which is very realistic. You can live a life filled with successes if you abound in knowledge and surround yourself with wise counselors. Most people are destroyed because of their failure to get knowledge, failure to seek counselors and failure to adhere to knowledge without a vision. *"My people are destroyed from lack of knowledge.* *"Because you have rejected knowledge, I also reject you." (Hosea 4:6)*

Retiring at age 49 from the U.S. Army came with quarters in an annuity and disability income, along with significant health benefits. Early on, there was a lack of appreciation on my behalf for the difficult and sacrificing years of making a descent income. This attitude carried over to not staying out of debt, nor refusing the unbelievable plastic credit card marketing campaigns. In time and painfully, my health quickly reminded me of the great need for respecting the value of the dollar. Which led to establishing a detailed budget and financial scorecard for all spending, saving and investing of each quarter. These valued quarters were planted and watered by my wife and me through nurtured stewardship and respect, which were transformed into dollars. Changing our financial attitudes blessed us and the anointed monies grew and bore a bountiful harvest. We learned to live in the Lord's desired abundant life, which you can have through good works and discipline.

It is the Lord who can give increase, not man, machine or your will. Favor and increase under grace must be His Will. You are to be hot or cold, not lukewarm in being disciplined stewards. Never have a craving or love for money, for this attitude and behavior will cause you to make numerous mistakes. You must embrace wisdom and get understanding in dealing with money, for your attempt to protect wisdom is like valiantly trying to protect money. The advantage of getting knowledge, wisdom and understanding in all things is that only by being wise can your life be preserved, even if you do not have wealth. *"Simon, Simon, Satan has asked to sift all of you as wheat.* *But I have prayed for you, Simon, that your faith may not fail." (Luke 22:31–32)*

Money has its purpose and value, but it also has its share of problems and leads some to destruction, even death. When well used with knowledge, wisdom and understanding for life's needs to be met and for the purposes of living a quality life, money will be well spent. But when money takes on a careless attitude that drives you into believing money can afford a life separate from God and equal with God, the travesty is defeat, loss and spiritual death. Money is simply a tool created by God to take care of the needs and provisions of life needed for the earth and humankind. God does not need the money, but He does need us to be wise and learn from one another in the Spirit of Christ to be good stewards of the monies He blesses us with. Therein, if you have wise advisors and coaches, you can be wise with your monies, whether large or small, or paycheck to paycheck. For the purpose is to preserve your monies for your needs. The first charge is to give a generous and bountiful portion unto the Lord, for the upbuilding of His Kingdom. *"Wisdom is a shelter as money is a shelter, but the advantage of knowledge is this: Wisdom preserves those who have it." (Ecclesiastes 7:12)*

"A good person leaves an inheritance for their children's children, but a sinner's wealth is stored up for the righteous." (Proverbs 13:22)

Circle of Experts & Advisors Model

AREA	CIRCLE OF EXPERTS & ADVISORS
1	Confidant, Conscience and Purpose Mentor
2	Biblical & Christian Living Mentor
3	Principles, Values and Morals Mentor
4	CPA and Tax Lawyer Advisor
5	Family, Estate, Criminal and Real Estate Lawyer Advisor
6	Financial, Banking and Business Advisor
7	Retirement and Wealth Planning Advisor
8	Real Estate and Mortgage Advisor
9	Marriage, Family, Life and Relationship Coach
10	Career and Executive Leadership Coach (Civilian, Federal, Military, Entrepreneur, Business)

ANTIDOTE 19 |
TAKE CARE OF YOUR QUARTERS

"Live life focused on enjoying today, with balance and visions of your future." Erogies Grigley Jr.

Does your lifestyle rob you of financial freedom? Life should be embraced and lived to the fullest, not being robbed daily by regrets and bad decisions. Although money is not everything, wealth is the answer to everything in life applied to living above your environment and born conditions. If you live from paycheck to paycheck or cannot make ends meet each day, your life is exposed to mental and emotional anguish and daily defeat to have a quality of life. Not being a good steward of your monies is as dangerous as not having monies come into your life. *"Give generously to them and do so without a grudging heart; then because of this the Lord your God will bless you in all your work and in everything you put your hand to." (Deuteronomy 15:10)*

Embrace a lifestyle to live under your means, inside the Dollar Allocation Model. Invest early, consistently and over time. Keep pace and conversations with your Circle of Experts & Advisors, as they will pour knowledge, wisdom and understanding into you. Your quarters will accumulate if you value and wisely use them. Never discount the seriousness of counting your quarters before you receive them and having a direct plan for accounting for and maximizing each quarter. Embracing this principle and applying its core values – stewardship of financial peace, financial independence, financial lifestyle and financial wealth – become a realization, highly likely and favorably possible! *"Whoever can be trusted with very little can also be trusted with much." (Luke 16:10)*

Regardless of the amount of money you earn, if you fail to give thanks to the Lord and have no stewardship, the canker worms, caterpillars, grasshoppers and locusts will come. The same exists for your desire to live more abundantly and to leave an inheritance will also be devoured. Once gone, once removed from your treasures, once spent, you cannot get the quarters back.

Every quarter is too difficult to amass in dollars, for you to easily let them be swindled away. And, the adjoining lifestyle potentials that the quarters offered before losing them are also gone forever. You must compare how many hours, labor, time and energy it takes to make your money. For example, if it takes 20 hours at a rate of $25 per hour to make $500, you must include travel, gas, and actual hours on the job to appreciate all that comprised the $500. If it takes one hour to spend $500, it will take you 20 hours to make that $500 back, above the 20 hours you normally work. This understanding should bring enlightenment to the level of time, energy, and costs it takes to make money, compared to how easily you are willing to spend it in less than an hour.

You can make new quarters quicker than you can make new dollars, but if spent or given to another, the spent and given away dollars are lost forever! Decide if you want to be poor, live an unpleasant life, and allow ego and pride to cause you to envy others who took care of their quarters. Or, account for every quarter to be spent and control your spending to become a producer, not a lifetime consumer. Live for enjoying today, with work, rest and play balance, while focusing on the future and enduring a wonderful life with all needs met and provisions provided. *"But store up for yourselves treasures in heaven, where moths and vermin do not destroy, and where thieves do not break in and steal." (Matthew 6:20)*

Find something you love. Discover the love affair of a financial challenge. Embrace what you would do for free. Then, you will find your vocation and perhaps your purpose and potentially be handsomely rewarded. At the very least, you will enjoy the works of your hands, mind, spirit and heart, daily.

Usually, the importance of coins rides low in pockets, gets tossed in bowls and piggy banks, you name it. Coins accumulate for years. Some people tell employees to keep the change of coins. Why are coins viewed as having less value than their younger sibling, the dollar? What must you do to realize your quarters can propel you to being debt free, financially independent, and for a few, wealthy, if invested properly? The quarter is only of less to no value to the person who does not value money in general. This person also does not value a budget or financial scorecard. If they did, they would embrace and value the rule, "I tell my money what to do before letting it do what my desires would have it to do".

Every quarter has value and when combined and multiplied, placed in a financial institution, the quarters do something that is magical, no miraculous... they turn into dollars! Have you received a mind shift, a revelation on valuing the monies you earn? The phrase is widely known: *"For the love of money is a root of all kinds of evil"* (1 Timothy 6:10) and *"Yet my people have forgotten me...which made them stumble in their ways..."* *(Jeremiah 18:15)* As they wandered from the principles and faith in the Source, they find themselves overwhelmed with many despairs and heartaches.

What must be done to change this phenomenon? Be discipline and have a specific and detailed plan to account for and maximize each quarter before you receive them. Regardless of the amount of money you earn, make or receive, worldly people will always seek to devour. The same exists for your desire for peace, quality of life, liberties, freedoms and opportunities to live more abundantly and to be able to leave an inheritance are also devoured. Once gone, once removed from your treasures, once spent, you cannot get these quarters back. They are too difficult to amass to amount to dollars for you to let them be stolen. *"Keep your lives free from the love of money and be content with what you have, because God has said, 'Never will I leave you; never will I forsake you.'"* *(Hebrews 13:5)*

These tenants and lifestyles beloved friends are the secrets to life's successes. Always surrender to giving your best and demonstrating excellence in all things, going after what you set your mind to with zeal and great faith. You may only reach the skies and not touch a star, but this will be a small step for you, but a giant step for your life and future with God. Do not concern yourself with defeated and undiscipline people and them telling you what to do and how to do it. Listen to and walk with the Lord, as He is perfect in all things and undefeated in everything.

This reflection must become your constant attitude that eclipses every condition of old. For it is the Source who fills you with new prophetic epiphanies. You must focus on what is needed, in glorifying God and with great labors, works, and compassions! As the scorn confines some to being "boat talkers and not water walkers", they are confined to natural laws and not the divine laws of God. Beloved, just move towards Christ's will! *"Act according to whatever they teach you and the decisions they give you. Do not turn aside from what they tell you, to the right or to the left."* *(Deuteronomy 17:11)*

Never co-sign on a loan for anyone, for anything! You become responsible for the loan if the other party defaults. Never loan a person your quarters who mishandle and devalue their quarters, as they will never repay you the loan. How can they, if they cannot manage their own quarters? Only give a quarter to someone here and there, now and then, who actually tries hard, values their quarters and uses stewardship principles wisely. But, only give away what will not affect your quarters, Dollar Allocation Principle and accumulation towards financial independence. You should only lend or give away quarters that you can afford to give away without impacting your lifestyle and stewardship allocation. *"If anyone is poor among your fellow Israelites in any of the towns of the land the LORD your God is giving you, do not be hardhearted or tightfisted toward them. Rather, be openhanded and freely lend them whatever they need." (Deuteronomy 15:7-8)*

Show compassion for those who use their quarters wisely to prioritize purchasing what they need and got to have. Do not give quarters to those who use their quarters to purchase what they want, then beg to borrow someone else's quarters to buy what they need. If you seek the Lord first in prayer and supplication in all things, you can become an abnormal and spiritually strong vessel as a friend of Jesus Christ and be known as an influencer and producer. As you freely choose to value planting and harvesting your quarters to invest in fertile soil and watering with prayers, wisdom and visions are given from the Holy Spirit. Then, the Source promises the quarters shall multiply and increase, little by little. Help others who are less fortunate and in true need, not want. You can put yourself in a highly probable position to retire early, and not have to work until you turn 65 to 70 years old with these wisdoms and Antidotes. For more information, see the Dollar Allocation Model in Antidote 17.

Once you have captured your finances and budget using the Dollar Allocation Model, you must address your financial concerns and income earned. Reassess life issues for good decision-making to achieve the highest and best results with your Circle of Expert Advisors. Then, tell your quarters and dollars where to go based on facts and the best advice received. You must focus on having five or more income streams coming into your home. These can range from careers, a business, rental property, second retirements, annuities and a second job. *"Invest in seven ventures, yes, in eight; you do not know what disaster may come upon the land." (Ecclesiastes 11:2)*

Remember, most people have poor and lower perspectives and little to no enlightenment when it comes to valuing money, talents, gifts and time. These people have resorted to living from paycheck to paycheck, with no monies in the bank, fail to tithe a portion back to the Lord and cannot offer to help anyone. This type of person frequently spends their entire paycheck on what they want; then they find others to borrow money from to meet their needs. You who are enlightened, disciplined and who follow *The Art of Living Well* as a way of life, will never beg for bread and milk, will not become the borrower, but the lender, who live in abundance. You must see a thing as it is and call out the thing as it is, and when you see a person in wisdom as to who they are, believe your eyes. Do not lessen the thing you see in a person to become a victim of being used by them. Clarity will always show them in their true form, and either they will pay what is due, or otherwise fail to pay and will result in eviction. You cannot allow your mind to be clouded with foolish emotions that lead to poor decisions with money. This will lead to no value added and you will punish yourself with greater losses from the acceptable risks you created!

The Dollar Allocation Principle accounts for each penny and forces the quarters to be allocated before they arrive in your bank account. After you have told your quarters where to go, no one can tell you what to do with your quarters or ask for your quarters. You must prioritize and direct your quarters to take care of you in the present and in the future.

"Wisdom, like an inheritance, is a good thing and benefits those
who see the sun. Wisdom is a shelter as money is a shelter,
but the advantage of knowledge is this: Wisdom preserves those who have it."
(Ecclesiastes 7:11-12)

ANTIDOTE 20 |
NEVER MAKE
EMOTIONAL DECISIONS

"Most of one's difficulty exists in the weakness
of the carnal mind, which gives way to fleshly desires and perceived
wants and needs, becoming trapped in the pitifulness of making
you the victim of one's on doing." Erogies Grigley Jr.

Have you made a decision that later grieved you greatly and you needed
life to take a different turn, for the better? Each new day comes with a
new joy or new challenge. Life holds a myriad of ups and downs, but your
better days should be greater than your bad days. This determination is
in the foundation of your choices. *"Choose my instruction instead of silver,*
knowledge rather than choice gold, for wisdom is more precious than rubies, and
nothing you desire can compare with her." (Proverbs 8:10)

You must never allow yourself to be placed under futile pressures,
under foolish demands or overwhelmed with negative stress when at all
possible to avoid. There are good stresses, which can positively challenge
and lead you to great and wise decisions. This positive stress usually comes
in the form of preparation, performance, anticipation and meditating
on the outcomes before reaching a climatic decision or discovery. You
must make your decisions while in a sound mind and never in Significant
Emotional Experiences (S.E.E.).

The pressures and negative stresses of this Antidote concentrates on an attacking and paralyzing mental, spiritual and emotional phenomenon. One which seizes your reasoning and heart into a catastrophic paralysis or a regretful life impacting nightmare. You will either come to your senses or wake up the next day and ask: "How in the 'hell' did I get to this horrid and desolate place in my life?" You do not have to look far to see the collateral damages of finances, family, friends, and even faith. And for many, defeat and utter destruction is realized, in a matter of minutes or hours, not days or years when the monsoon and cyclone hits from negative stress decisions. *"David said, 'My son Solomon is young and inexperienced, and the house to be built for the LORD should be of great magnificence and fame and splendor in the sight of all the nations. Therefore, I will make preparations for it.' So David made extensive preparations before his death." (1 Chronicles 22:5)*

Exercising silence is usually the correct answer, especially when emotions are running high, selfishness is ramped, and confusion is abounding, as the threat is real and imminent! The difficulty for you to face and embrace unexpected loss from a bad choice or grave decision becomes a shocking reality. Your dismissal in the denial that the typhoon of life was reported earlier simply make matters worse. You could see the evidence that the typhoon-like conditions of uneasiness and indifferences were building, the shifting and colliding winds within your emotions were howling, the rise of 40-foot waves of perplexing mental attitude and shifting uneasy anxieties were hitting harder every day. Yet, you ignored the apparent and reticence of factual formations of hurt which were building rapidly. This is done to avoid the forces generating negative stress or simply to remove yourself from the conditions of the tornado's path. In the end, failure to act and a last-minute futile attempt to make a wise choice under duress is far too late and a costly price must be paid. Never, never, regardless of the price up front, can one afford to ignore all the signs and fall victim to other's voices and demands, and wait to make a critical decision. Especially, when facing or going through a Significant Emotional Experiences (S.E.E.), especially with your quarters, dollars and relationships with others. You must protect your quarters and dollars, as well cover and guard your relationships, peace and harmony of life. Perilous results are often considered and preventable before they happen. *"You must act according to the decisions they give you at the place the LORD will choose. Be careful to do everything they instruct you to do." (Deuteronomy 17:10)*

When important decisions are made or even greater in a S.E.E., the ideal moment of resolution can and usually will be lost forever. Once the collision occurs, the cyclone or monsoon hits, you are in no position of authority to act with reason that will make a difference. Everyone involved directly and indirectly risks befalling to the perils, which will devour all in its worldly path. But when you gird your loins victory can be achieved. These are done at the expense of someone's feelings being hurt and emotions being placed in check, under tough love and facing the plan called life.

In the absence of facts, prayer and patience during a S.E.E., the expected positive outcome has already been greatly diminished. You are apt to suffer defeat and depression, and even ruin. Moreover, you will find yourself outside of the Will of God, as you operate in your will and lean to your understanding, removing the Lord from the process for abundant living. *"Trust in the LORD with all your heart and lean not on your own understanding; in all your ways submit to him, and he will make your paths straight." (Proverbs 3:5-6)*

The difficulty exists in the weakness of the carnal mind. This gives way to your perceived wants and needs, trapped in the pitifulness of making yourself the victim of your on doing. Exercising silence is rarely the correct answer, especially when emotions are running high, selfishness is ramped, and confusion is abounding, as the threat is real and imminent. Silence can prove to be a paralyzing falling away of friends and family, and even develop into a deadly poison of bitterness and resentment that cannot be recovered from, for which there is no antidote. Have the courage and boldness to call a thing a thing. Hold the violator and the victim responsible for their individual and collective actions, or lack of actions. This is the only way for truth and righteousness to avail. You can become your own worst enemy when you allow emotions to drive your actions and reactions to a thing, person or event. A rational person cannot have a conversation with an irradicably selfish person or fool and expect a rational conversation and outcome. Many times, it is best not to bring yourself down to the lower level of emotional combustion and foolery. This will cause you to rebuke or be rebuked but feeling worse for letting go of your peace. *"Do not rebuke an older man harshly but, exhort him as if he were your father. Treat younger men as brothers, older women as mothers, and younger women as sisters, with absolute purity." (1 Timothy 5:1-2)*

You must remain of sound mind and hold fast to mature judgment when facing the storms. You must be as a ship built for storms, for when the storms come, your ship will not capsize or breakup, for the Lord is on your side. You survive, because you have demonstrated faithful trust and stewardship over that which you have been blessed with. You are a ship to transport the Lord's love, ways and Word; therefore, as His ship, He built you to handle the frustrations, challenges and tests that will come from the world. He also gave you the believer as a wonderful Helper. To lead, guide and direct your thoughts and ways along the path of life for your journey towards His purpose, which is your goal and truth. *"Be diligent in these matters; give yourself wholly to them, so that everyone may see your progress. Watch your life and doctrine closely. Persevere in them, because if you do, you will save both yourself and your hearers." (1 Timothy 4:15-16)*

Eating too much P.I.E. (Personalize, Internalize, Emotionalize) which others have made, even your own, can be hazardous to your health, spirit and mind. Be careful with this, for eating too much can be contagious! You must not develop an appetite and addiction in eating too much

P.I.E. to cause an emotional roll-a-coaster of faults. Avoid hearsay or perceptions from mental gymnastics that only exists in your mind. Wisdom must test her facts and understanding, which will require constant forgiveness. When you focus on and consume P.I.E., you are actually focusing on fear and insecurity. When fear and P.I.E. collide, this causes anxiety, depression, insecurity and confusion to rob you of life's precious commodities – time, trust, quality of life, joy, happiness and excellence of peace. *"Be careful, or your hearts will be weighed down with carousing, drunkenness and the anxieties of life, and that day will close on you suddenly like a trap." (Luke 21:34)*

Never personalize, internalize or emotionalize the issue at hand. When you do, too much is read into a matter. You may have heard the person but did not listen correctly to what was said. The simple matter of conversation becomes a mountain of stress and confusion, usually over nothing or a misunderstanding. Emotional experiences can offer some good, however, not when conducting business or making critical decisions. You must be in possession and have total command of your heart and reasoning when it is time to be decisive in making moral decisions. As surely as you live, there will come a time where the quarters and dollars you labored for will be needed. Especially for the matters of reality, too include the known and unforeseen which are surely to come, as certain as the sun rises in the East and sets in the West.

The secrets in this avoidance are simple: 1) The decision to be made must come with time to ruminate and study the matter, to gain knowledge, wisdom and understanding first; 2) Run quickly from anyone or a situation involving your time and monies that require you to purchase today; 3) Never let someone tell your quarters and dollars where to go, what to do and when to go. You earned the dollars and you alone with the wisdom of the Creator should determine where they will go and how they will be spent. If you honor your work ethics and your study, you will appreciate your sacrifices and successes. You must be careful in how you see things and who you let into your space, as you take care of your quarters. *"Starting a quarrel is like breaching a dam; so drop the matter before a dispute breaks out."* *(Proverbs 17:14)*

Critically important is to let your 'Yes' mean 'Yes' and your 'No' mean 'No' with a wonderful sense of joy and peace in your being and mind. As you mature to saying 'No' more often, your yes's will become less, and your instincts will rise to lead and guide you in foresight and insight. You will be able to reduce your nurturing desire to be an enabler, limiting your failing hindsight, headaches and fights with your mate. Prevent loaning money that will return void and spending money on something not needed that will cause waste. These financial and monetary acts were unnecessary, preventable and simply foolish to acquire and loan away monies you do not have or should not give, only to cause such pains and toils. Do not be lukewarm with being responsible and accountable, in all aspects of your life. Learn the beauty of saying 'No' to worldly desires and 'Yes' to your heart desires which are in God's Will. For then, you will receive favor for whatsoever is in God's Will. *"Let your conversation be always full of grace, seasoned with salt, so that you may know how to answer everyone."* *(Colossians 4:6)*

Essential to your decisions for a funded life of joy, peace and freedom is simply stewardship, discipline and obedience with monies. It does not matter how much money you bring home, but rather how much of the money you save and invest. Stewardship requires an assessment of your behaviors and habits that require change and discontinuing, as well as new habits that add value to your financial portfolio and funded life of joy, peace and freedoms. When there is failed stewardship, the failure will come with grief, disappointments, missed opportunities, mounting bills, missed payments, collections and a downward spiral of your credit score. Heartbreak will come because of the conditions you have created for yourself and your whole home. Stewardship, not just financial management, is a path to success in all areas of life that require obedience, discipline and consistency, coupled with the simple word "works". The greater your stewardship, the greater the expected rewards both in the moment and in latter days. Your present acts create opportunities for ownership (home, investment properties, dream car) and streams of income.

When you meet the Lord on the sea, will you say, *"Lord, if it's you", as Peter replied, "tell me to come to you on the water." (Matthew 14:28)* What do you do? Step out the boat praying in the spirit, closing out the naysayers and scornful ignorant demands of the boat talkers with fear? Put your toes on the water and keep your eyes on the Lord. For you hear His voice and when He asked you to come to Him, you are immediately identified as a water walker. You are to exercise your faith in the evidence of what you see in the supernatural and walk not on water, but the divine highway, which the Lord has put in place. People that are boat talkers should not even rise to be your friends, only the water walkers should be, for they trust you, are compatible and want the best for you. By these words, void of fear, certain acts of faith are in conflict with boldness of actions in the carnal minds and cannot focus on miracles witnessed by God. You can operate in the spirit with great faith, and the Holy Spirit will lead you to step out of the boat filled with fear and boat talkers. You must not concern yourself with what is, but rather with what can and will be in the Spirit of the Lord, as a water walker. For it is He who bided you to come to Him, standing on divinity, which belongs to Him, and He is Christ, the Source of all that is good and perfect.

Never walk in your own ways, or use worldly speech, or say whatsoever pleases your pride, ignorance and flesh. These habits create the foundation to form lustful behaviors of the world that do not make you complacent to sit in the seat the greats have set in, which becomes their counsel. Stay vigilant and on guard against these prideful thoughts, for their principles and thoughts will seduce you into false premises of immortality and invincibility. They produce and display selfish motives for greed to promote self and most assuredly, they are jealous of your rise in success, nobility and virtues. They will attempt to bring scorn in all they own and do. They desire to take away your peace and joy, as well your greatness. It is imperative to know and embrace that God is without limitations and bears all weakness, thereby giving you strength in your greatest challenge and strife. Stay connected to the Source! Never settle for complacency, for its sole purpose is to focus all your energies on doing nothing and being held back. It takes ten times the energy to do nothing, over the energy to exercise positive and joyful initiatives and actions daily, towards measuring your life's daily successes unto God and bettering your life! *"Because you have raged against me and your insolence has reached my ears, I will put my hook in your nose and my bit in your mouth, and I make you return by the way which you came." (2 Kings 19:28)*

All decisions you make are free will with some level of influence from others. The most important influence, however, should be found in prayer and communion with Jesus Christ. Prayer will never lead you astray or waste your time with the Lord, for in Him rests all truths, wisdom, knowledge, understanding and determination. You are reminded not to lean to your own mental gymnastics and logic for understanding. Embrace the above tenants and tools, but in getting the above, you are to get crystal clear understanding and direction from Christ before you move on actions through prayer and sometimes fasting. Sometimes you must be reminded that in the Scriptures you must be true, honorable and righteous. God requires such character for His blessings to go forth, when you who are called by His name as His own. You must humble yourself, pray, turn from your sinful ways and seek the Lord first. Listen, then will He incline His ear to hear your voice from heaven and answer your prayers. *"If my people, who are called by my name, will humble themselves and pray and seek my face and turn from their wicked ways, then will I hear from heaven, and I will forgive their sin and will heal their land." (2 Chronicles 7:14)*

His Word shall go forth with power to accomplish the very thing for which it was purposed: to heal the one who is in need and cover and bless the home and land to which the Lord has given you. Stay wise and pray unceasingly my friend!

"Do not show partiality in judging; hear both small and great alike.
Do not be afraid of anyone, for judgment belongs to God.
Bring me any case too hard for you, and I will hear it. And at that time, I told
you everything you were to do." (Deuteronomy 1:17-18)

ANTIDOTE 21 | DO WHAT YOU HAVE TO

"The strength to do what you have too, must be in the honorable will of the Lord for your life to be favored and pleasant to live." Erogies Grigley Jr.

Has the hand you were dealt in this life caused you to live beneath others and limit your choices? Are you living an honorable life that is pleasing unto the Lord? Does your faith and gratefulness align to God's loving kindness and faithfulness? God's desire is for you to live a joyous and good life. But many of the tests and trials you have to go through cause you to question the life you live. You cannot live in evil or for others and expect your best interests to be foremost. *"For it is better, if it is God's will, to suffer for doing good than for doing evil." (1 Peter 3:17)*

Some people live to eat, and others eat to live. In this later life, I have learned to do the latter, which disrupts a weak attitude and increases a focused discipline. The Lord has always been with you, even before the world was created, as Scripture records in John 1:1, *"In the beginning was the Word, and the Word was with God, and the Word was God."* God and the Lord Jesus are one, inseparable in their relationship to lead, guide and favor you to live abundantly. He wants you to be filled with joy and peace, towards a long life. A life of promise and longevity, and for your descendants to transcend your life, generations upon generations.

All that you do must be tempered and measured against your heart and spirit, aligned with the righteousness and glorification of the Lord in both doing and living, a life pleasing unto the Lord. You cannot live to rely on your devises. For surely out of your fleshly pride you will believe it is by your power and might that great things are done. This is buffoonery, where not only do you fool yourself, you become distant to God and out of right alignment. You run the risk of everything you possess and work hard for falling to thieves or ruin. *"They have become filled with every kind of wickedness, evil, greed and depravity. They are full of envy, murder, strife, deceit and malice. They are gossips, slanderers, God-haters, insolent, arrogant and boastful; they invent ways of doing evil; they disobey their parents; they have no understanding, no fidelity, no love, no mercy." (Romans 1:29-31)*

You must rise early mornings embracing your passion for life and purpose for living, in truth and righteousness, and honorable to your first love who is Christ. Your first ministry is family. Sometimes this ethos challenges your personal necessities for making you first. When you make the first step towards your vision to be the greatest you, the momentum of your resilience becomes the action which moves you closer to living the way you want to, yet noble, honorable and pleasing unto the Lord. Make the most of time to do what you have to, as the earth is full of beauty, yet most beauty remains unseen. If not careful, you will continue inhabiting days covered with a world of people that desires your soul. Their wicked eyes of ego, pride, power, control and greed will pursue you to place you in shackles to monetary debt and participating in sin with them. Draining you for the lifeblood to sustain capitalism and their self-worth for more money. Not only do they count and not take care of their quarters, they count yours and make you work to increase theirs. These people will also scheme and rob you of opportunities for passive and intellectual income. Be a producer and not a consumer in this life.

Your eyes must be vigilant, senses must be keen, spirit must be fervent in steadfast prayer and the mind must sacrifice and submit to the Spirit of the Lord, according to His voice and known Word. When this occurs, with total surrender, trust and faith, the Lord will deliver you from your plight, place you on a firm foundation and give you surpassing peace and abounding grace in all things, and all of life. A strong supportive position in Scripture records, "For *I know the plans that I have for you,*" declares the Lord, "*plans to prosper you and not harm you, plans to give you hope and a future.*" *(Jeremiah 29:11)* The Lord will do what He says!

The Lord desires you to measure life in days, with the mind of God, not in years with man's thoughts for years are fleeting and difficult for accountability. In spirit, seek to measure your daily life in height, width, length and depth for gains and successes, to understand the Lord's Will for your life and pleasing Him. Do not be foolish; rather, get knowledge, seek wisdom and get understanding to ensure His ways are your ways and your journey is filled with His purpose along the Lord's path for your life. Be of sound mind, filled with the Spirit of the Source, not filled with intemperance, envy, laziness and a yearning for pressed grapes daily. You cannot expect an old wine bag to hold new wine without ripping apart! You must exercise initiative to improve and stay the true course towards increasing aspirations and accomplishing goals and achieving high honors. *"Command them to be good, to be rich in good deeds, and to be generous and willing to share. In this way they will lay up treasure for themselves as a firm foundation for the coming age, so that they may take hold of the life that is truly life." (1 Timothy 6:18-19)* This is the way to success!

You must be very vivid to distinguish your visions and aspirations. Make plain your dreams into goals by hand of penmanship, to create testimonies unto and of the Lord's sovereign hand. Be diligent and have the great resolve to start what you yearn for and finish strong what you started. Each small success represents building blocks that will be used for realizing greater successes to build the house that God promised. Stay committed to your vision and ensure you meet each day with zeal to do great things. Make the vision come to past and marvel at your faith, and His faithfulness with helping you do what you have to, to live the way you want to. However, the vision must be of God's Will to be lasting and strong to stand against hurricanes and storms, trials and tribulations, which will surely come. As you understand that the Source is not a respecter of person, and does not favor one who is lukewarm, He will bless whom He chooses. The Lord does whatsoever is His Will; therefore, take no thought to envy or jealousy, never desirous of another's wealth and material things. *"Write the revelation and make it plain on tablets, so that a herald may run with it." (Habakkuk 2:2)*

You must rise early mornings embracing your passion for life and purpose for living, sometimes opposite of your necessity in the moment and season for being able to provide for basic needs and pleasures. Make the most of the time the Source and Creator gives you to do what you have to under the authority of the Source and those He places over you. *"Pray for us. We are sure that we have a clear conscience and desire to live honorably in every way. I particularly urge you to pray so that I may be restored to you soon." (Hebrews 13:18-19)* In surrendering to Christ and exercising humility to be under the rule and counsel of those placed over you, at home, career and life, there is wisdom and successes to be had. Those over you are responsible to Christ to guide your journey with provisions and wisdom for understanding to live an abundant life. In ministry and family, these are the very ones responsible to watch over your soul for eternal life and Kingdom living in this life. Know that you are to always remember and respect those over you, for the Creator speaks through those in authority. *"Remember your leaders, who spoke the word of God to you. Consider the outcome of their way of life and imitate their faith. Jesus Christ is the same yesterday, today, and forever." (Hebrews 13:7-8)*

Christ is also the provider of your provisions, manifested through those He appoints for your benefit. If you allow Him, He will illuminate your path and guide you into understanding and the way in which you should go for an abundant and joyous life. Christ will fill your life with provisions from a career and income needed for life. This is accompanied with a wonderful place to call home, filled with laughter and someone special to share it with. *"Your word is a lamp to my feet and a light to my path. I have taken an oath and confirmed it, that I will follow your righteous laws. I suffered much, preserve my life, LORD, according to your word." (Psalm 119:105-107)* Be mindful of the schemes and wickedness of the evil one, whose eyes of ego, pride, and greed are stayed on you. Stay on the path of life, so you are not taken captive and placed in chains mentally, physically, financially and spiritually.

You can learn from those who have already experienced success in ministry, business, career, marriage, parenting, writing books, etc. Wise counsel is a necessity before applying your mind, tongue and hands to anything. For there is nothing new to be discovered or done that the Source has not already created in Heaven as it is on earth. Therefore, do not think you are full of wisdom beyond your years or beneath your education. Christ is the Source to all things under the sun and under the heavens. Everyone who is under His authority is also used as spirits with the Holy Spirit to control the blessings that come around you and upon you, that is in keeping with His Will. *"For lack of guidance a nation falls, but victory is won through many advisers..." (Proverbs 11:14)*

Continue in spirit to seek to understand the Lord's Will for your life and pleasing Him. Do not be foolish; rather, get knowledge, seek wisdom and get understanding to ensure His ways are your ways and your journey is filled with purpose along the Lord's path for your life. Be of sound mind, filled with the Spirit of the Source, not filled with intemperance and envy. You must exercise the initiative to improve and stay the true course towards accomplishing your goals.

Make your dreams plain and into goals to create testimonies unto the Lord's sovereign hand. Be diligent and believe that you will be successful. Have the great resolve to start well with what you yearn for and finish strong what you start. As you understand that the Source is for your good, you will embrace He will bless whom He chooses. He selects solely and simply for His Will to become the unmerited power in your purpose, which is His Will for God's glory and your blessings unto self, family and others. You must be hot or cold, dependent on your environment and not sitting on a fence aloof, crying in your lemonade or laying around watching time go by as you are glued to the worldly temptations of the internet and television.

Conditions and scenarios will always exist for comments and concerns of others who fail to understand your drive and pressing long hours as your means to an end. They want what you have, but aren't willing to do what you have to, too live the way God wants you to. Feel the exhilaration of being exposed to the vivid pictures painted in your mind and see what is on the eve to come from the Lord, by staying the course, persevering and making necessary sacrifices in faith , when others choose to give up. Your tongue is a double-edged sword with the capacity to bring life or death, which are your own. Does not your strength, time, common sense and fortitude come from the Lord, the Source and Creator, who are Lord over us? As such, you should realize that the only power another person can have over you is the power you freely and willfully give, or the power God gives to them for His purpose which may or may not be revealed to you.

If you are in a pleasing and righteous relationship with the Lord and chase after His heart with a repentant spirit and heart, He shall hear and answer your prayers through forgiveness and favor. Who, then, can say they are powerful enough to contradict God and control you? Only you can give an account for your life to the Lord, who favors the righteous. He knows these people of His are weak, but in your weakness is where the strength of God resides and increases to bring honor unto your name. Only let the Source guide you in any endeavor that you shall receive a just reward and Jesus will be pleased and glorify His Father. He will require something of you, which may be of trials, tribulations, suffering, pain, loss and even delaying the vision. Once His Word goes forth it goes forth with power and dominion to accomplish the very thing for which He purposed it, for those that love Him, and His Word cannot come back to Him void. *"And my God shall meet all your needs according to the riches of his glory in Christ Jesus." (Philippians 4:19)*

Be content with the blessings the Lord graces your home with for a quality life. It is the Lord who chooses to give some people greater wealth, possessions, peace and honor. These people seem to lack nothing and receive everything their hearts desires, without concern for their neighbor or compassion for others. If you show patience and watch carefully, you will discover that the Source grants anyone He chooses with the wealth of joy and happiness. Most people with wealth wrap this accomplishment around their heart, making this their treasure. And the Lord never grants them the ability to enjoy their labors because they do not have the Lord first in their lives. Fall to your knees and pray, then rise and do works of excellence. Does not your strength, time, understanding, wisdom and fortitude come from the Source and Creator?

If you are in a pleasing and righteous relationship with the Lord and chase after His heart, He shall hear and answer your prayers through mercy and grace. Let the Source guide you in every endeavor, that you shall receive a just reward and He will be pleased and glorify His Father. God requires for you to be discipline, obedient and trusting with an abiding faith that produces trust and His faithfulness to your life. Pray a prayer of faith and belief that once His Word goes forth it goes forth with power and dominion to accomplish the thing for which He purposed it. *"I have been crucified with Christ and I no longer live, but Christ lives in me. The life I now live in the body, I live by faith in the Son of God, who loved me and gave himself for me. I do not set aside the grace of God, for if righteousness could be gained through the law, Christ died for nothing!"* (Galatians 2:-20-21)

These tenants and lifestyles, beloved friends, are the secrets to life's successes. Always surrender to giving your best and demonstrating excellence in all things, going after what you set your mind to with zeal and great faith. Pursue accomplishing successes that you reach beyond the skies and touch a star, letting this be your drive to live the way you want to. Do not concern yourself with people telling you what to do and how to do it. If you are walking with the Lord, you know that He is perfect in all things and undefeated in everything. This reflection must become a constant, as you heighten your senses towards overcoming every condition of old, as the Source fills you with new knowledge, understanding and wisdom. This embracement moves you closer along the path for treasures. Which includes joy, peace, prosperity, wisdom and love for living the way one wants to, having done what one needed to do. The scorn is confined to being "boat talkers", and they are confined to natural laws. They will never embrace the divine laws of God for their conversations and responses to His urgency to move. Do something, beloved. If you do not do anything else, get up and pray!

When the Lord says to you, "I bid thee to come to me," what will you do? Step out the boat praying in the spirit, closing out the naysayers and scornful ignorant demands of the boat talkers with fear and keep your eyes on the Lord. When He asked you to come to Him, you were immediately identified as a water walker for the purpose is to exercise your faith in the evidence of what you see in the unknown and walk on the divine highway. Friends can either be positive depositors in your life or robbers of your peace, joy, happiness and strong now faith. By these words void of fear, certain acts of faith are in conflict with boldness of actions in the carnal minds and cannot focus on miracles by God. You can operate in the spirit with great faith, and the Holy Spirit will lead you to step out of the boat filled with the fear of the boat talkers and not concern yourself with what is, rather what can and will be in Spirit of the Lord. For it is He who bids you to come to Him, standing on divinity, which belongs to Him, and now you in great faith and focus can walk and speak with authority over all things with boldness. *"Come to me, all you who are weary and burdened, and I will give you rest. Take my yoke upon you and learn from me, for I am gentle and humble in heart, and you will find rest for your souls. For my yoke is easy and my burden is light." (Matthew 11:28-30)*

Stay vigilant and on guard against these prideful thoughts, for their principles and values. They produce and display selfish motives for greed to promote self and most assuredly, they are jealous of your rise in success, nobility and virtues. They will attempt to bring about scorn in all you own and do, to take away your peace and joy towards experiencing greatness, which is impossible in the Lord. It is imperative to know and embrace that God is without limitations and bears all weakness, thereby giving you strength in your greatest challenge and strife. Stay connected to the Source! Never settle for the easy and give to complacency, for complacency and disbelief's sole purpose is to focus all your energies on doing nothing and being held back to be nothing. It takes ten times the energy to do nothing, ten times more than to exercise initiatives and actions daily, towards building successes and measuring your life daily unto God and doing kingdom business for humanity!

"Pray for us. We are sure that we have a clear conscience and desire to live honorably in every way. I particularly urge you to pray so that I may be restored to you soon." (Hebrews 13:18-19)

ANTIDOTE 22 |
MAKE SURE YOU
ARE HONORABLE

"Fill your cup with the foundation of knowledge, wisdom,
understanding, and exercise your mind with patience to build
the framework of reasoning, in all things, for all things."
Erogies Grigley Jr.

How should you respond to betrayal? How should you respond to the trappings of mind and spirit? How should you respond to culprits that rob you of joy and value? No one is exempt from experiencing pain, loss, disappointment and trappings of betrayal. However, everyone can limit exposure to being placed in a submissive attitude and trapped condition of hopelessness. *"For we are taking pains to do what is right, not only in the eyes of the Lord but also in the eyes of man." (2 Corinthians 8:21)*

Without hesitation, you must evict people who does not pay living and mental rent, and causes debt, foolishness, betrayal, grief, and depression! Allowing such behavior will usher in disappointment, loss of joy and peace, and even regrets. The change or effort, in actions or words must add value, not take away and degrade from what already positively exists. Whatever the choice and decision, you must ethically and morally own it in spirit, heart, mind and soul.

You must determine risks and added value and not give way to the influence of someone else shifting your perspectives, principles, values, purpose and truth. You must be strong and embrace tough love, not eat too much P.I.E. (Personalize, Internalize, Emotionalize) and never play mental gymnastics with your mind, spirit and heart. Do not live in your emotions and feelings, rather live in the present in truths. Have a humble heart and gentle spirit set on a northern azimuth using the lodestone to fill your cup with the foundation of knowledge and wisdom and exercise your mind with understanding. You must have patience to build the framework of reasoning in all things. Call a thing a thing; don't be deceived by looks or distracted by a passing light. Rather, demonstrate agape and philias out of all the loves, but always be vigilant to exercise valiant tough love in your decisions. *"Since you are precious and honored in my sight, and because I love you, I will give people in exchange for you, nations in exchange for your life."* *(Isaiah 43:4)*

Work towards building your life on a set of morals and ideas, with aspirations that are the foundation upon which you breathe, live and are willing to die for, if necessary. There must be a measure of standards to your purpose and perspective in the treatment of others. Resist the notion and abnormity to live a worldly life with its fads, pressures to give into, self-preservation to lie, steal, hurt, deceive and even destroy others. For the purposes of self-indulgence and self-gratification, to stroke your ego and to hold on to your pride. The very notion to always place yourself first and never consider the well-being of others is the first fallacy towards self-denial, lack of self-esteem and a path to self-destruction, rooted in pride, greed and conceit.

These thoughts promote a dangerous way of thinking. This form of selfish thinking builds upon formations of greed and manipulation, which will entertain the curiosity of sinful acts. When the acts become routine occurrences, habits are formed and these selfish and deliberate pre-meditated learnt habits grow into repeated conditions of acceptable experiences, called behaviors. Once the indignant behavior is entrenched, you become the unscrupulous, unmerited and lost dark knight and black sheep who suffers inwardly. You lose self-awareness and self-esteem, while rapidly shrinking to attempts to covering your deceit, divisiveness and defrauding others without conscience. *"When the woman saw that the fruit of the tree was good for food and pleasing to the eye, and also desirable for gaining wisdom, she took some and ate it. She also gave some to her husband, who was with her, and he ate it. (Genesis 3:6)*

The very veil under which the misbehaving person hides is to conceal their wayward spirit, heart and character. People with characters comprised of questionable reproach and coldness of heart are of no value-added to others or themselves, let alone to humanity and community. When you do not live with a high sense of honor, virtues and ideas, there is an absence of commonality of thought and cause for life. Therein, individual purpose and humanity of decency towards people are the realizations that the person is not worth living and offers no promise to life and tomorrow, for which the Lord is no respecter. You should cease to respect the existence of the flawed person as an intricate part of building and fostering life. Avoid them, until they come to their senses and succumb to the Will of God. This change will make them a better friend who is principle-centered and humble, no longer narcissistic.

Ethical and moral decision-making is not difficult if you make this perspective and principle a way of life, which embraces truths and the Lord's ways and thoughts. The ethical and moral decision process can be daunting, if you did not grow up in a home of values and morals. This principle simply refutes immoral and illicit behaviors that violate the principles and values: Obedience, Respect, Loyalty, Trust, Honor, Nobility, Reliability, Courage, Self-Discipline, Compassion, Self-Esteem and Servitude. Your core values and ethos are the sound fundamental beliefs that build the character of a strong foundation. Ethics and morals must exist in the person, in order for the family, community, team and climate of a home and community are to be effective and integrated towards a vision and shared mission. Below is a questionnaire to guide you in your ethical and moral decision-making.

Ethical and Moral Decision-Making Process

1. Is this action or deed the Will of God?

2. What positive outcome will result if I do this?

3. What negative outcome will result if I do this?

4. What positive outcome will result if I do not do this?

5. What negative outcome will result if I do not this?

6. Will Jesus Christ be pleased, and God glorified if I do this?

7. Will Jesus Christ be displeased, and God not glorified if I do not do this?

8. Will I help someone if I do this?

9. Will I hurt someone if I do this?

10. Can I lay down in peace and rise in joy if I do or do not do this?

Your ethos and core values are the guiding principles that dictate your behavior, actions and reactions, for added value. Making ethical and moral decisions are paramount to how you live. *"Finally, brothers and sisters, whatever is true, whatever is noble, whatever is right, whatever is pure, whatever is lovely, whatever is admirable--if anything is excellent or praiseworthy--think about such things." (Philippians 4:8)*

Spiritual wisdom and divine knowledge entwined in the anointing of the Source and Creator are the single internal azimuth that goes beyond conscious and subconscious thoughts. This is a necessity to form more perfect decisions for self and others. Your core values and ethos are simply that which define your character, beliefs, name and word. These life sets will help you achieve purpose and success with peace and joy and can help other people to know what is right from wrong. Living this way is absolutely critical in the pathways of rules, expectations, and values at home and in the community. Embracing this belief can help leadership support children and neighbors, in determining if they are on the right path towards fulfillment of their vision and goals. You must find ethics and morals in lifestyles, to ensure creating and fulfilling your purpose, and embracing your truth. You must travel the path of your journey with an unwavering perspective of enlightenment and not become weary of fainting or quitting what you started. *"Do not be hasty in the laying on of hands, and do not share in the sins of others. Keep yourself pure." (1 Timothy 5:22)*

Ethical and moral decision-making must be earned and developed over time and through experiences, as well as training and education, undergirded by beliefs and betterment causes toward humanity. These are at the core of relationships and determining what is most important – the priorities, respect and trust, especially in a marriage and family. I have learned and experienced the difference between going on a date and courtship, when listening to the people I mentor and discussing what were the reasons they fell in love with their husband or wife. Consistently, all couples express that they were compatible and shared the same values, focused on trust, communication, loyalty, respect, humor, aspirations, nurturing and being in a courtship, which led to love. These lead to the spiritual fruits of joy, peace, compassion, intimacy, respect and a healthy life of family, individual quality of life, inspiration, career satisfaction, and vacationing in the balance along the path's journey. Ethical and moral decision-making simply are not selfish or self-centered, but rather are servitude and principle centered in righteousness, honor, just and good. *But if you will seek God earnestly and plead with the Almighty, if you are pure and upright, even now he will rouse himself on your behalf and restore you to your prosperous state. Your beginnings will seem humble, so prosperous will your future be." (Job 8:5-7)*

What is added value? Neither people nor corporations can be successful without core values involving vision, mission, priorities, ethics, ethos, goals, leadership, trust and execution. Added value is the excellence of a positive person and making simple the complex, with simple positive actions which contributes to influencing change, growth and direction. Added value does not always have to be positive; sometimes added value can be negative. The negative added value can go against the majority or the strong winds pushing you into a storm. This is done in order to identify a better way or more efficient and safer outcome. Your personal moral azimuth's lodestone will guide your principles and values northward to benefit the whole, never just for self. Christ did not come to be served or to be king; rather, He came to save, serve, restore and be of servitude spirit and to give abounding grace and unwavering faithfulness in unconditional love. *"Whatever you have learned or received or heard from me or seen in me-- put it into practice. And the God of peace will be with you." (Philippians 4:9)*

In this life, you are to submit to wisdom, virtues and compassion for people and good will. Live life in higher ideas and giving of self towards selfless positive outcomes for family, friends and even strangers. Strive to resist the temptations of the world to concede living a life embolden in the activities that degrade and debilitate your fellow man and woman, boys and girls. You must embrace that only together, depending on one another, together in Jesus Christ, can you live in the hopeful fullness of abundant living on this fragile earth. Mother Nature is strong, formidable and has a long memory. She is also gentle, peaceful and forgiving if she is treated with dignity, respect and appreciation, above and beneath the surface. So, too, is man and woman, boys and girls, as everyone desires to belong. All want to be respected and appreciated for who they are as human beings.

Regardless of your position in life, it is shallow and reprehensible to not live with a high sense of honor and decency towards people. It is paramount and of sheer proportionate resolve for every person to embrace that every life is worth protecting. And, you should enjoy living. *"And walk in the way of love, just as Christ loved us and gave himself up for us as a fragrant offering and sacrifice to God." (Ephesians 5:2)*

This selfless surrender to make others better offers great promise for a harmonious life and future tomorrow with great and abiding hope for everyone. The respect for each other, the respect for self, the respect and gratitude to the One to whom each one belongs should stir a great surge of climatic enlightenment for the rightful existence of a person. You should be thankful for being a part of life and to contribute in small steps for humankind and gigantic leap for the Source and Creator. If only one person teaches this to another, and this one embraces the teaching, now two can teach four, four forty and forty can teach four hundred, and for hundred reach four thousand, who can teach the world, in perpetuity. Embracing this Gospel enables God to reach the world to embrace the Sovereignty of the Lord and the fullness thereof that reside in yourself, yet while you live and grow.

"Acquitting the guilty and condemning the innocent—the LORD detests both of them. Why should fools have money in hand to buy wisdom, when they are not able to understand it? A friend loves at all times, and a brother is born for a time of adversity. One who has no sense shakes hands in pledge and puts up security for a neighbor. Whoever loves a quarrel loves sin; whoever builds a high gate invites destruction." (Proverbs 17:15-20)

ANTIDOTE 23 |
EMBRACE LIFE'S
PRIORITIZATION PRINCIPLES

"There is no food for the soul that man can produce;
such does not exist in the physical or natural to help one do everything
with order and well-being." Erogies Grigley Jr.

Have you wrestled with any decision in life for something you so desperately wanted? Do you want to live a greater life, but do not want to spend the money? There is no sustenance for the soul that man can produce without being of the spirit, linked in the fullness of the Holy Spirit through Jesus Christ for well-being. There is always the Source, Christ and His Word, with His Holy Spirit, truths and principles of Spirit, which are enriching and fulfilling foods, spiritual nourishment for the soul with pure peace and strong joy. *"But seek you first the kingdom of God, and his righteousness; and all these things shall be added to you." (Matthew 6:33)*

You must determine the what, why, when, where and if something is a 'Want', 'Need' or 'Got to have it'. In simple language, the Prioritizing Principle is used to establish if it is a:

- Want – an immediate satisfaction to engage in emotions, desires and lusts, that leads to greed;

- Need – a requirement for meeting human needs, a necessity to acquire or engage in specifics for dealing with a problem to ensure your needs are fulfilled;

- Got to have it – a critical act required for living, safety, security, justice, freedoms and liberties with protection of family and assets.

There is a stark difference between a believer's and unbeliever's faith in the Messiah, the Source, which some are diabolically opposed to prioritizing life's 'Wants', 'Needs' and 'Got to have its'. Believers refer to your faith and the Lord's grace, mercy and love when growing weary in this life. Opposition challenges you daily, even though you only have the Scriptures and a promise from Jesus Christ to rest on, as you know He came and will come again. He is a very present help in the midst of life's challenges and complexities. Not only this, but He returned to heaven to sit at the right hand of God on the Mercy Seat. His second coming to earth is absolute to give one the fortitude in full countenance to believe and wait for Him, while doing good and pleasing works along the path of life, in His Will and for His love. The unbeliever continues in his plight of recklessness towards satisfying both a prideful mind and a greedy heart. The unbeliever refers to self and remains diabolically opposed to *the art of living well* in the Source and Creator, relying on self and living for self, at the expense of others. There is no love, trust, discipline, honor, grace and mercy where the unbeliever lives! *"And God is able to bless you abundantly, so that in all things at all times, having all that you need, you will abound in every good work." (2 Corinthians 9:8)*

The price is a ransom paid in full by the Creator, using the Source as full payment for the remainder of your earthly and eternal days. You are pardoned and past wrongs and sins are forgiven and hid from God's face. The price Jesus paid assures that you as a believer will be with Him in Paradise and live with Him spiritually one day. Soon, you will be with Christ in the new city called Zion. There you will know the full measure of being a part of the royalty of the King and His Father. If it is not a 'Got to have it', you should be cognizant of what your hard-earned monies are spent on. Specifically, if the purchase or investment is not in God's Will, it may simply be a 'Want' or 'Need' expenditure.

The cost is a required submission and obedience from you for the remainder of your days in *the art of living well* earthly and spiritually. The benefits and perks of surrendering to Christ heavily outweigh and broadly reach beyond the eyes, for such brief happiness. The cost requires denying yourself for Him and giving up the things of old that are not of His Will and laws. You are led to put others before you with compassion and care, with restraint and reasoning. This aim is for those that are truly humble and trying hard to live a good and pleasing life to the Source and Creator.

If you fail to apply the Prioritization Principle, the significance of life's essentials (food, home, clothes, education, peace, joy, health, quality of life, banking and love) could go missing and lacking. The world and Mother Nature will do it for you with great pain or take away with great loss. You will reluctantly come to the conclusion that worldly people's unwillingness to embrace living abundantly will come at a high price. If you are involved with them, they will cause you to pay a preventable price and painful cost to bear. For many, such as you, may choose not to make exceptions or apply the Prioritization Principle because of your status in life.

I am reminded in the earlier Antidote of people's difficulty to amass dollars and some let their money be swindled away easily. The opportunities that the dollars offered before losing them are also gone forever. You must compare how many hours, labor, time, energy and costs it takes to make your money. Earlier we discussed that if it takes 20 hours and at a rate of $25 per hour to make $500, including travel, gas, and actual hours on the job, the value exceeds $500. If it takes one hour to spend $500, it will take 20 hours to make that $500 back, above the 20 hours you normally worked, and the ancillary costs involved. This should bring enlightenment to the level of time, energy, and costs it takes to make and keep money, compared to how easily you are willing to spend it in less than an hour. Simply, money's cost and labor are too great to continue embracing an abusive attitude of stewardship that does not protect your hard-earned monies. *"This is a trustworthy saying. And I want you to stress these things, so that those who have trusted in God may be careful to devote themselves to doing what is good. These things are excellent and profitable for everyone." (Titus 3:8)*

Study and take copious notes on the promised Redeemer and Messiah's coming, where His divinity was covered in flesh to be born through a virgin to dwell amongst us as the Source and the Vine. His divine appointment and free will choice to do God's Will was life altering, critical, essential and unparalleled altogether as a 'Got to have it'. He freely gave the spiritual and moral laws and covenant to be available to all in order to offer free salvation and receive His faithfulness. He took the sting out of death and took the keys to eternal life after death from the evil one. He overcame fallen angels from heaven to give believing people the free will choice to be saved from a corrupted and sinful world. You are guaranteed a new covenant founded on His better promises, abundance and an eternal spiritual in heaven after life's journey comes towards an end. This covenant leads to the final destination along the path towards the endeavors of His purpose and your choice. Jesus's coming as the begotten Son of God is, was, and will always be a 'Got to have it', even after the end of time.

Use the Antidotes in this book as wisdom to tell your mind and heart what to do for God, yourself, family and humanity. If you do not have Antidotes available, who can you provide Antidotes to? First, exercise living within or beneath your means of income. Take care of your family as your 'Got to have' ministry. Limit primary spending of money, talents, gifts and time only to 'Got to have it' requirements, which are critical for survival in life. A safe home to live, food, water, clothing, emergency savings, tithes and offerings, helping others, quality of life and peace of mind, unto the Lord are a 'Got to have it'. Jesus promised, fulfilled all and has given faithful witnesses full reports and a living record of His existence and promised return. Limit secondary spending of money, talents, gifts and time only on 'Need to have it' things that meet requirements necessary for improving living, what is at hand to improve careers and plans for the future, and an inheritance to move you closer to God. *"That is why the Levites have no share or inheritance among their fellow Israelites; the LORD is their inheritance, as the LORD your God told them." (Deuteronomy 10:9)*

Limit fleeting optional and gratification choices in spending money, talents, gifts and time only on 'Want to have it' things that provide for an improved life, entertainment for balance in life, mental shifts in vanity and decoration of one's outer appearance. Too include uplifting self and the family, taking vacations and to feel high self-esteem to give hope for living an abundant life. If you are obedient and discipline as a good steward, live within your means and are pleasing the Lord, you will live a more abundant and pleasing life, before men and God.

If you embrace these tenants, the Prioritization Principles and compartmentalize spending money, you will have more to show for what you earned, and you will find success. Proper use of one's valuable time and gifts with the spirit and truth, and being ethical, will place you on the path towards distinguishing differences if something is a 'Want', 'Need' or 'Got to have it'. Exercising this discipline can best be achieved by using the Life Mapping Matrix. You can get this resource by contacting the author from his website. This resource was designed with a decision-making plan, inclusive of key data, facts and assumptions for direction and prioritization of life with viable and realistic courses of actions. You can use this model to build a foundation for abundant living along the path's journey with confidants and friends, guided by the Lord, in *the art of living.*

"Our people must learn to devote themselves to doing what is good, in order to provide for urgent needs and not live unproductive lives." (Titus 3:14-15)

ANTIDOTE 24 |
ARE YOU READY TO GO TO WAR?

"One must embrace purpose and cause on earth, to be light and not live in darkness, be good salt and not sand, and be courageous and not fearful, to live abundantly." Erogies Grigley Jr.

What do you do when your wants and needs outweigh your priorities in life? Do you principally, financially and mentally go to war with self? Life is filled with days of pain and years of joys, but our good days should outweigh our bad days. During the challenges that are faced, we are to weigh what is important and a priority. Many people fail to make their life necessities priorities, which leads to challenges and confusion. *"Take my yoke upon you and learn from me, for I am gentle and humble in heart, and you will find rest for your souls." (Matthew 11:29)*

Before committing to W.A.R. – Willing, Able and Ready – you will face decision points that must be addressed and defined in great detail. You must define the problem and purpose to your wants, needs and got to haves – which are influenced emotionally, mentally, physically and by family. These are critical points for guiding the decision-making process to achieve a definable and congenial status.

The same should apply to personal 'Wants', 'Needs', 'Gots to have it'. Before making a purchase, you must see light in facts and wisdom and not live in darkness. Be good salt and not sand and courageous and not fearful.

To be good salt, you must prove that your character is aligned to the Source and His Will. Do not focus on what is in it for just you and only your capacity and capability to achieve something. You must embrace the three tenants of W.A.R. – Willing, Able and Ready – or the outcomes shall be those of regret and failure, which will likely take shape, before the great fall and pride is humbled. However, to everyone else you are deemed a fool for placing the needs of others above your own. Listen to open, factual and wise counsel, but only embrace wisdom that comes with understanding and positive outcomes, based on everyone is Willing, Able and Ready to move forward towards purpose and truth in God's will. *"Let us not become weary in doing good, for at the proper time we will reap a harvest if we do not give up. Therefore, as we have opportunity, let us do good to all people, especially to those who belong to the family of believers." (Galatians 6:9-10)*

Never purchase major items under heightened emotions. Stay clear of riches from greed and material possessions gained off the backs of others. Such as, opportunities of network marketing, multilevel marketing, and pyramid and Ponzi schemes that promise you your ship is coming in. You will be taken for a horrible journey off the well-traveled path. If you do not adhere to this warning, be prepared to lose friends and part with family members. Never commit to something unless you are Willing, Able and Ready to see it through. Ask yourself: "Am I willing to do this without reservations?" "Am I able to do this financially and have the support of my spouse, family, friends, colleagues and boss?" "Am I ready to do this mentally, emotionally, spiritually and physically with the necessary time, energy and resources?" *"Be joyful in hope, patient in affliction, faithful in prayer. Share with the Lord's people who are in need Practice hospitality." (Romans 12:12)*

If you can say "Yes" to each question, then proceed with caution and zeal. If you answer "No" to any of the questions, do not proceed with the event or activity. This includes other people's money, time, talents, gifts and energy as well. Such examples would benefit from the W.A.R. analysis when purchasing or upgrading a car or home, starting a business, investing in a mutual fund, changing jobs and careers, traveling, going on vacation, or purchasing a timeshare. If "No" is chosen, you have taken a strong position against an opportunity. If you are pressed with making an immediate decision, it automatically falls into the "Not W.A.R." category. Save yourself invaluable money, time, frustrations, headaches and troubles from scoffers and leeches by simply being spiritually discerning and aware, and therefore feel good to say "No"! Regardless of how appealing and attractive the deal looks, or the persuasive charming and pressurizing talk continues, the answer remains a resounding "No"!

Give due diligence and steadfast prayer on every move you consider making and every dollar you plan to spend. Therefore, know that the Source will be on your side, preventing you from making a grave error and gigantic mistake. *"No", they replied, "there may not be enough for both us and you. Instead, go to those who sell oil and buy some for yourselves." (Matthew 25:9)*

There will always be a falsehood created by those who are scoffers. You will deceive yourself if you become a victim. You must deflect the foolish argument that they embrace. You can achieve W.A.R. for what appears to be a great deal. W.A.R. will always reveal the major falsehood of scoffers' arguments and detect the lies and signs of being setup for betrayal. Observe where the scoffer and leeches' approach with a smile, open handshake, and well dressed. They come offering semi-expensive snacks with a false sense of complete desire to be fair, honest and looking out for your best interest. They appear overly confident and advise there have been many before you that saw the opportunity and made the deal. Don't do it! They are bold enough to say that the company has not made any changes in years and this is the first time they decided to increase the benefits and reduce the prices.

Remember that W.A.R. is designed to prioritize life's spending and reduce hurt and disappointments based on a set of principles and morals, not emotions. Keep W.A.R. in your forefront, discuss "No" before going shopping, on the visit or during the visit. If you were not Willing, Able and Ready to make the deal or purchase, feel good that you will not be negatively impacted. Shy away from these things in your life. Steer clear of the scoffers and leeches. Be firm and bold in your voice to take a stance, saying, "I am not interested. I will not!"

These scoffers and leeches are so overconfident that they will always overlook those who are filled with values, principles and understand W.A.R. and the Prioritization Principle if the something is a 'Want', 'Need' or 'Got to have it'. They will take no consideration of your inner makeup and these tools will go unnoticed. Although, they might ask questions to get hints of who you are relative to character and core values, they are not looking out for your best interest. They will be so engulfed in themselves and their pitch, that they will be oblivious, even though they ought to have known your position and character. Yet, because of greed and the love of money, they willingly are ignorant of the fact you have already gone through your W.A.R. and priority analysis and simply choose to pass over their greed in silence. *"Keep your lives free from the love of money and be content with what you have, because God has said, 'Never will I leave you; never will I forsake you.' So we say with confidence, 'The Lord is my helper; I will not be afraid. What can mere mortals do to me?' " (Hebrews 13:5-6)*

Those who are foolish will play along with a purchase or possible major expense as a game. They will act as if they never heard or know anything like this deal before. If they did, they will likely get trapped by the smooth fast talking and make a foolish decision to purchase or invest. The unwarranted and foolish act is likened to failure to retain knowledge and tools; for they did not embrace the W.A.R. and Prioritization Principles. Rather, they fell in love with the emotions of ownership or having a sense of false pride and vain conceit. At this point, you did not care that they took advantage of you. The focus was for you to own something you did not need or could not afford; or was simply unwise to acquire, devaluing your hard-earned dollars and quarters.

I discovered how difficult it is to persuade people to hold on to their dollars and live for a higher cause. Many are ignorant simply because they do not take the time to research. They do not follow or use the tools given to them. Or, maybe they are unwilling to embrace discipline spirits to become knowledgeable and apply the tools of living abundantly. Pride often gets in the way, as they are ignorant of not knowing what they do not know, thereby are not able to make sound ethical-decisions or wise choices. Never act on emotions to do anything involving money, family and your future, for you will exercise ignorance or waywardness in the mind. If ignorant people crucified the Lord Jesus Christ, you should be on your guard for sinful natured people to exercise their carnal minds to financially and emotionally crucify you. They will use your ignorance and culpableness as excuses for helping you get rid of your money and committing you to a lifelong financial obligation of a deep dark pit. You simply are throwing your good hard-earned money into a black hole with no possible return on investment. I stand corrected; you also gain headaches, arguments with your spouse and your self-esteem crumbles before you as you look in the mirror and look at your dwindled bank account. *"Rejoice with those who rejoice; mourn with those who mourn. Live in harmony with one another. Do not be proud, but be willing to associate with people of low position. Do not be conceited. Do not repay anyone evil for evil. Be careful to do what is right in the eyes of everyone. If it is possible, as far as it depends on you, live at peace with everyone." (Romans 12:15-18)*

Now, proceed with full confidence in *the art of living well* and the wisdom and enlightenment contained herein. Use life's tools and skill sets to do everything through vetting, while using W.A.R., Ethical and Moral Decision-Making Model and the Prioritization Principles. I would be remised to not mention that you have God on your side and the Lord has proven His worth in your life beforehand. When you act on 'now' faith and steadfast prayer, God operates on Sovereign power and faithfulness to help you. Thus, do not dismiss the Lord from being a part of everything in your life. He makes no mistakes, and He will lead you spiritually towards success and overcoming scoffers and leeches. Be slow to make a decision to go to W.A.R. without careful consideration for possible loss. In the future, use the Prioritization Principles for all decisions, and determine if you are 'Willing, Able, Ready', in conjunction with the Ethical and Moral Decision-Making Model, if it is a 'Want', 'Need', or 'Got to have it'.

"Or suppose a king is about to go to war against another king.
Won't he first sit down and consider whether he is able with ten
thousand men to oppose the one coming against him with twenty thousand? If
he is not able, he will send a delegation while the other is still
a long way off and will ask for terms of peace." (Luke 14:31-32)

ANTIDOTE 25 |
CHESS FOR LIFE. CHECKERS FOR FUN.

"Life and the world will rise to test your spirit, mind, heart, body, fortitude, faith and love through ole' giants and young wolves."
Erogies Grigley Jr.

Is your life filled with daily battles of facing giants, wolves and vultures that takes you off the journey you imagined for your life? Life's journey takes many turns and the days can be filled with distractions, depression and disaster, if the focus in not on the Source. The battles faced can range from self-inflicted pain, financial and mental attacks to threats from foes and heavy spirits from friendly fires. *"Since we live by the Spirit, let us keep in step with the Spirit. Let us not become conceited, provoking and envying each other." (Galatians 5:25-26)*

In your journey along the path towards your destiny, not your destinations, the world and enemies of God will certainly form weapons to use against you. You must be prepared to face these challenges to survive and live with power and authority over all enemies that prepare snares and fiery darts and arrows against you. Because of your godly walk and wholehearted faithfulness in the Lord Jesus Christ, these weapons cannot prosper to harm you. There must be a clear and vivid determination and defining of the people that want to lead you astray. But, fret not. Stand where you are as God holds your hand and gives you a spirit of discernment armed with the sword, His Word, and clothed in the fullness of His armor. Both the world and even some people within the church will give a united effort to seduce you away from the Will of God for your will and their will to be done. Some will rise as they are, and others will be dressed in arrays of clothing as lambs, puppies, doves, and even children. *"They come to you in sheep's clothing, but inwardly they are ferocious wolves." (Matthew 7:15)*

There is joy, peace and strength to go around or above the storms and to battle the lions, bears, wolves, vipers and locusts. These victorious living attributes are found in the wise strategy for your visionary outcome. Be decisive with wisdom and courage to express "checkmate" in chess and equal excitement in the move and expression to "king me" in checkers. Such are the parallels of living and mastering chess matches to be successful against humankind fears, isms, discriminations and phobias. You should learn the art of playing checkers to find balanced quality of life! Always seek wisdom, knowledge and understanding to have dominion authority and reverence power over your enemies in all things and all days. The Lord requires you to not be ignorant of His power, might and Spirit, for it is the Source that gives you all that is needed to know when to play chess or checkers.

Chess comes into existence in your career, workplace, finances, finding a good wife or an honorable husband, raising children, mentoring and coaching others. The chess experience is also found in the church, being responsible for others, and exercising gifts and talents that result in saving, protecting and helping people. This is greatly influenced in church ministry, where the pastor is responsible for preparing, protecting and preserving the souls of others for Christ.

The chessboard consists of 64 squares combining eight rows and eight columns and 32 various and different pieces in different colors, sizes and materials. Each square on the board has a name from A1 to H8. The same applies in life with different people, in color, race, ethnicities, cultures, thoughts, goals and isms. The chessboard squares are arranged in two alternating colors of dark and light. While different materials vary widely, there exists different classes of people by status throughout the world. Usually, wooden boards are commonly used in high-level games. Plastic and cardboard are common for low-level and informal play. Only ones with superior skills get the opportunity to play on chessboards of decorative glass and marble. However, these materials are normally not accepted for sanctioned games, as these games come with rewards and costs. So, too, does life. Usually the privileged can afford the better and more desirous quality things in life – peace, joy, family, home, clothing, cars, jewelry, vacations, etc. But, in the Source and Creator, all prosperity is highly potential to have if it is a part of the Lord's Will.

There is great responsibility and accountability for different amounts of time and seasons that require great reasoning and testing. Nevertheless, you have to exercise the great power granted by God on your life which must be used for God to bless His people who are called by His name and those that love Him. Through you and being clothed in spiritual armor with great 'now' faith, you can do all things through the Source, Jesus Christ. *"Now faith is confidence in what we hope for and assurance about what we do not see." (Hebrews 11:1)*

However, you cannot have lukewarm faith and small works. Your opponent will trap your king in less than five moves. You must understand the game and your opponent's personality profile, character traits, different chess games played, familiar strategies used and your rare moves from the Holy Spirit to defeat your opponent. Your opponent's defeat will come because you purpose in your heart and are equipped for the challenge. Before accepting the job, going into the game, mounting the pulpit, standing behind the lectern, or walking on the stage, you will have prepared for a time such as this. For an abundant life, you must exercise leadership and applying the Word of God to live for the Source and use your gifts for God's glory.

Checkers come into play during your daily walk, mostly evenings and weekends, to live carefree and spend time with family and friends. You may not play chess, or even be great at checkers. However, you should realize that in either the chess match or checkers game you cannot afford to be ignorant of your surroundings and competition. But with great study, learning, faith and prayer, you can be victorious. The black and white, or black and red checkerboard of 64 alternating squares is covered by opposite colored chips lined across the board. Does this sound familiar? In America and most countries, separation is by black and white, brown and white, the haves and have nots. In this game, you can make moves across the 64 squares (8×8) of alternating dark and light color, often black and red vertically and diagonally as a move. The same applies in life in our 36-square inch brain (6×6) when faced with balancing family life. You should have fun playing checkers and living, but reasoning is still required to understand the rules of the game and strategies that can be deployed to achieve living abundantly.

Checkers command attention and pace for your next move and your opponents' possible moves, with some forgiveness for an error being made. Chess commands attention, tactic, patience and meditation, as every piece on the board outweighs pace and relies on strategy. Every possible move and countermove come with risks and can lead to checkmate, quickly. The same level of thought, patience and preparedness must accompany you in your life as you live to lessen attention and counter life's moves of opposition. God commands your attention to obedience to His Word and love towards all for your daily life, even towards your enemies. This is hard, but achievable as the years mature you and your character is led by the Spirit of God. *"For if you live according to the flesh, you will die; but if by the Spirit you put to death the misdeeds of the body, you will live. For those who are led by the Spirit of God are the children of God." (Romans 8:13-14)*

The Lord knows the plans for your life, which are to prosper you and give you a life of longevity under the heavens and on His earth. You are reserved for great works and great rewards, which your family will inherit in the Lord. You must learn to play both games, chess for life and checkers for fun, while remaining focused on earlier principles and *the art of living well.* It is recorded that one day with the Lord is as a thousand years, and a thousand years as one day. *"But do not forget this one thing, dear friends: With the Lord a day is like a thousand years, and a thousand years are like a day." (2 Peter 3:8)*

You can have great expectation for long days that amount to a short life comparatively, 70 to 80 years or 25,550 to 29,200 days to one's life. *"Our days may come to seventy years, or eighty, if our strength endures; yet the best of them are but trouble and sorrow, for they quickly pass, and we fly away." (Psalm 90:10)* When you measure life in days and not years, the reality of this psalm becomes more relevant. You become more alert to live your abundant life in perspective and principle. In simple conversation, you ought to master playing both checkers and chess, living and working, while maturing. Play both often to challenge your mind and strategize your behaviors in living. Also, play both to have fun and enjoy the art of playing. If you do this, you will always experience less bad news and more happy moments, less losses and more gains, less strained relationships and stronger and trusting relationships, with less separations and divorces, and more lasting marriages for life. These come with less rebellious children and more obedient and enlightened youth to adults.

Finally, I am reminded of the Scriptures in Matthew 25 as Jesus enlightened the disciples through exhortation on being watchful of His glorious return. Everyone will have to give accountability of personal actions and deeds to Him, to those who were least, but in need of help.

Jesus related that the commandment of these acts done or not done for Him are equal and treated the same if done to the least of those in need. He requires selfless acts of commitment in visiting, serving, feeding, clothing and compassion to render agape love to the sick, poor and lowly of heart. *"They also will answer, 'Lord, when did we see you hungry or thirsty or a stranger or needing clothes or sick or in prison, and did not help you?' He will reply, 'Truly I tell you, whatever you did not do for one of the least of these, you did not do for me.'" (Matthew 25:44-45)*

In summary, Christ brings great clarity to His expectations and instructions while providing righteous and agape believers with expectations to be able to come to Him. You will become the blessed inheritors of the many rewards in the kingdom of heaven, set aside just for one's works and faithfulness. Christ was also sharp in tone for His warning that when you are not willing to do for those who have little, you isolate the fullness of your life from Jesus. In more direct purpose, Christ is saying for you to show compassion and love for your fellow men and women, boys and girls by sharing what He has blessed you with in abundance. When you give out of your abundance to others in need, Christ will cause increase and overflow. You will give out of His generous portion, and you can be honored to keep the abundant portion, not missing anything or being without, forever. As the blessings pour through you, the blessings also fill you!

Jesus informed the disciples in strong words of challenge and awareness that all will be judged for the effectiveness of action and the motives residing in their heart and in the life lived, according to obedience and faith. He continues with what, why and how you will be separated by the Judge, using the illustrations of sheep and goats, righteous and unrighteous, for the final judgment. It is your behaviors and motives towards or against specific agape deeds that identify the perfect or imperfect nature of a person. Your very deeds will be used to judge you before the Sovereign Judge, Jesus Christ.

"As a prisoner for the Lord, then, I urge you to live a life worthy of the calling you have received. Be completely humble and gentle; be patient, bearing with one another in love. Make every effort to keep the unity of the Spirit through the bond of peace." (Ephesians 4:1-3)

ANTIDOTE 26 |
NEVER MAKE A DECISION
YOU WILL REGRET

"People problems evolve from facts and assumptions ignorantly
understood, wrongly weighed, improperly judged,
poorly communicated, foolishly applied and greedily twisted."
Erogies Grigley Jr.

Do the problems in your life come from poorly weighed decisions? Are false assumptions and moments of ignorance surrounding your actions put into motion? During your lifetime, you are faced with thousands of situations and opportunities often receiving minimum attention. Then, there are life-impacting challenges and decisive moments which require heavily weighed decisions to be dealt with. *"Now I know in part; then I shall know fully, even as I am fully known." (1 Corinthians 13:12)*

The simplicity in achieving the best outcome for difficulties are found in decisiveness and clarity of your subconscious mind and heart, in spirit and truth. You should not exercise mental gymnastics of what is not, creating actions and events that do not exist. And, do not ignore the facts and consequences or rewards which will manifest in positive or negative outcomes when acted upon.

You can conclude with reason and probability that most human problems evolve from 'what can I get out of this'? Challenges are only correctly resolved through wisdom, understanding, prayer and sound rational actions taken from validated facts and true assumptions. You should try to live peaceably with everyone, while knowing the risks associated with these persons. You can use Erogies's Ethical and Moral Decision-Making Process and Model that was received by grace from heaven and the Holy Scriptures in Hebrews for making you better, wiser, spiritual and more mature in your personal relationship and conversation with Jesus Christ. *"In accordance with your faith if it is serving, then serve; if it is teaching, then teach; if it is to encourage, then give encouragement; if it is giving, then give generously; if it is to lead, do it diligently; if it is to show mercy, do it cheerfully."* *(Romans 12:6-8)*

It is essential to constantly revisit your core values, principles, ethical and moral decision-making, as the world will test you more often than expected. Along the path and in *the art of living well*, you who are higher in understanding and embracing wisdom and love discovers the simplicity of God's giving and caring for humanity greater. This understanding allows you to always be positive and optimistic, even in the midst of challenges and sufferings you must endure. It is paramount that when you are journeying this mature path towards the art of living, you must avoid manipulating others. Neither can you allow others to manipulate you, while you constantly give of yourself to others in the name of the Source. The giver is plentiful and bountiful and blesses those who are just and righteous in their ways, thoughts and deeds towards others. If you cover the spiritual gift placed into you by the Giver, who is the Source and Vine, your needs have already been met and your desires in His Will have already been given. Why? Because they are heavenly and divinely rich, wealthy and know they are in the Will of God and carrying out His purpose for your life. Money is important and answers many things, but the love and chase after money can lead to ruin and much pain, befalling to evil thoughts and ways. In all situations of choices and challenges, I assess myself on these values to limit and determine both my risks and level of risk acceptance. I confidently and Christianly refer to ethics and morals for my choices using my Ethical and Moral Decision-Making Process.

Problems, issues, difficulties and challenges are only correctly resolved through wisdom, understanding, prayer and sound rationale actions taken from validated facts and true assumptions between people. This is done knowing the risks for the future, as you live in the present with wisdom to prevent disasters and perils. You are encouraged to "Refer to the Ethical and Moral Decision-Making Process". This will help you make better and wiser mature decisions for a greater personal relationship and conversations with Jesus Christ. In all situations of choices and challenges, these values can be used to limit and determine your risks and level of risk acceptance and avoiding unacceptable risks. *Do you not know that we will judge angels? How much more the things of this life?" (1 Corinthians 6:3)*

There is a reason why your provisions and protections rarely require asking the Source for more. He always provides just what is needed and usually with overflow. The Will of God will not take you where His grace will not be present and tender new mercies towards His purpose for your life. His angels are forever present for ministering and warring all about you for protection. The Lord provides you with provisions and preserves you and your legacy, for the Lord's glory. *The art of living well* demonstrates having the attitude of greatness in the mind of God and living in spirit and truth. Then, you are truly set free through your new birth and emergence from the water and putting old things and ways in the past. Therefore, you must live above the laws of man and the laws given by God, living in grace and being holy, for God is Holy. You can live this life with the Lord in spirit and thereby live in the spirit realm more than the worldly realm of life. In this manner, the Lord is able to do exceeding and abundant things with you, for His Will. You do not need vast riches to be wealthy. Wealth is in health, mind, body, spirit, soul and relationships, overflowing with peace, happiness and joy! Choose to live in harmony with life and the earth, while honoring and reverencing the Lord, and you will be prosperous and have a long and good life. *"Who is wise and understanding among you? Let them show it by their good life, by deeds done in the humility that comes from wisdom." (James 3:13)*

Always revisit your core values and ethical decision-making, as the world will test you more often than expected. Along the path and in *the art of living well*, you who are higher in understanding and embracing love discovers the simplicity of God's giving and caring for humanity and self positively. Your journey along this mature path refrains you from manipulating others and prevents others from taking advantage of you, while you constantly give thanks to the Giver. You rarely require asking for provisions and protections, as God's grace will not take you where He will not be present and provide you with all that is needed for the journey.

You must never allow yourself to be placed under undue pressures with stress and make important life impacting decisions, especially with your quarters and relationships with others. You must protect your quarters, peace of life and quality of joy in life at all costs, period! Perilous results are often considered and preventable before they happen. When important decisions are made in the absence of facts or during a Significant Emotional Experience (S.E.E.), the expected outcome is greatly diminished.

The difficulty exists in the weakness of the carnal mind, which gives way to fleshly desires and perceived wants and needs, trapped in the pitifulness of making you the victim of eating too much P.I.E. (Personalize, Internalize, Emotionalize)! Never personalize, internalize or emotionalize the matter or issue at hand. Emotional experiences can be good for the heart and spirit; however, not when conducting business or making critical decisions relative to living well. You must be in possession and have total command of having quarters and dollars when needed, especially for the known and unforeseen which are surely to come. *"The mind governed by the flesh is hostile to God; it does not submit to God's law, nor can it do so." (Romans 8:7)*

You must not develop an appetite and addiction in eating too much P.I.E. to cause an emotional roll-a-coaster ride of committing errors and faults. People of sound mind must know the facts and test each other against the merits that they deserve and have earned in their sights, which will not require constant forgiveness. When you focus on the P.I.E., you are actually focusing on fear. When collided, fear and P.I.E. rob you of life's precious commodities – time, trust, quality of joy and excellence of peace in life.

You must consider that the secrets to this avoidance are simple: 1) The decision to be made must come with time to study the matter to gain knowledge, wisdom and understanding; 2) Run quickly, from anyone or a situation involving monies that require you to purchase today only – Ponzi schemes are perfect examples or an impulsive car purchase; 3) Never let someone else tell your quarters and dollars where to go, what to do and when to do it.

Reduce your failing hindsight, headaches and fights with your mate for spending money on something not needed, not a part of the financial plan, or does not fit in the budget and Dollar Allocation Model. Also, avoid simply foolish acts to acquire something not needed with monies you don't have. Stay wise, my friend!

You must rise early mornings embracing your passion for life and purpose for living, sometimes opposite of your necessity in the moment and season for being able to provide for basic needs and pleasures. When you take the first step towards putting actions with your vision to be the greatest you, your momentum moves you closer to living the way you want to. Make the most of time to do what you have to, to enjoy the beauty throughout the earth, because life is filled with a world of people that desires your treasures. Their wicked eyes of ego, pride, power, control and greed will pursue you to place you in chains. Their desire is to place you in bondage to monetary debt and participating in sin with them. Not only do they not count and do not take care of their quarters, they count yours and make you work to increase theirs. They scheme to increase the quantities of dollars you pay to them weekly, bi-weekly and for some, monthly for services and labors never rendered.

Your eyes must be vigilant, senses must keen, spirit must be fervent in steadfast prayer and the mind must sacrifice and submit to the Spirit of the Lord and His commandment according to His voice and known Word. *"Praise be to God, who has not rejected my prayer or withheld his love from me!" (Psalm 66:20)*

The Lord desires that you consider your actions in life towards His purpose. In spirit, seek to measure your daily life for gains and successes, to understand the Lord's Will for your life and that which is pleasing to Him. Do not be foolish; rather, get knowledge, seek wisdom and get understanding to ensure His ways are your ways and your journey is filled with purpose along the Lord's path for your life. Be of sound mind, filled with the Spirit of the Source, not filled with intemperance, envy, laziness, and a yearning for daily vises hazardous to your health. Exercise the initiative to stay the true course towards accomplishing goals and to achieve high honors. The height is your spiritual growth, the width is accomplishing your purpose, the length is the cause you have embraced, and the depth is who have you helped.

You must be vivid to distinguish your visions and aspirations from dreams into goals. Be strong and wise to start your vision, execute your strategy and persevere to finish what you start. Each small success represents key building blocks that will be used in the future for realizing many successes to build the house and family that God promised you, and that you committed to from a dream and a vision. Make the vision come to past and marvel at your faith and His faithfulness with doing what you have to, to live the way you want to. However, the thing, the act, the vision must be of God's Will to be lasting and strong to stand against life's hurricanes and storms which will surely come. As you understand that the Source is not a respecter of person and does not favor one who is lukewarm, He will bless whom He chooses. He selects solely and simply for His Will to become the unmerited power in your purpose, which is His Will, for God's glory and your blessings unto self, family and others. You must be hot or cold, dependent on your environment and not sitting on a fence aloof, crying in your lemonade or laying around watching time go by as you are glued to worldly temptations of the internet and television, and gossip. *"Pray for us. We are sure that we have a clear conscience and desire to live honorably in every way." (Hebrews 13:18)*

You must be willing to sacrifice what you want in the moment, to do what you need over time for a brighter future, and to live the way you want to. There will always exist conditions and scenarios for comments and concerns of others; those who fail to understand your drive and pressing long hours as your means to an end. You must feel the exhilaration of being exposed to the vivid pictures painted in your mind and see what is on the eve to come from the Lord, by staying the course, persevering and making necessary sacrifices, when others choose to give up. Be mindful of the double-edged sword tongues with the capacity to bring life or death on the sharpened sides, but never let this be your own, accept when you choose life.

Does not your strength, time, common sense and fortitude come from the Lord, the Source and Creator, who is Lord over us? As such, you should realize that the only power another person can has over you is the power you freely and willfully give to them; or, the power God gives to them over you for His purpose which may be revealed to you. If you are in a pleasing and righteous relationship with the Lord, He shall hear and answer your prayers. Who, then, can say they are powerful enough to contradict God and control you? Only you can give an account for your life to the Lord who favors the righteous. Let the Source guide you in all endeavors, that you shall receive a just reward. He will be pleased, and the Father is glorified by your obedience, faith and good works. He will require something of you which may be of trials, tribulations, suffering, pain, loss and even delaying the vision – even good works and blessings which you are to demonstrate sound stewardship. Once His Word goes forth you are blessed and favored with a promise. *"So is my word that goes out from my mouth: It will not return to me empty, but will accomplish what I desire and achieve the purpose for which I sent it." (Isaiah 55:11)*

"I have listened attentively, but they do not say what is right. None of them repent of their wickedness, saying, 'What have I done?' Each pursues their own course like a horse charging into battle. Even the stork in the sky knows her appointed seasons, and the dove, the swift and the thrush observe the time of their migration. But my people do not know the requirements of the LORD."
(Jeremiah 8:6-7)

ANTIDOTE 27 |
HONE A CHARACTER OF GRACE

*"The simplicity in achieving the best outcomes for the difficulties
faced is found in decisiveness and clarity of one's subconscious mind
and heart, in spirit and truth." Erogies Grigley Jr.*

When you are caught in a storm of life and feel defeated, how do you
respond and with what level of power? Everyone will experience challenges, trials and tests in their life, regardless of the season or their status.
The results of every storm is not bad or deadly. Storms can come against
you to build character. Storms can clear away old and cluttered to make
way for new beginnings and new growth. This comes with having a strong
foundation of trust and great hopefulness in the Source and Creator.
Tomorrow will come. Blue skies and rainbows will come, and your life
will be the better in Christ because of His grace and mercy. *"The Son is the
radiance of God's glory and the exact representation of his being, sustaining all
things by his powerful word. After he had provided purification for sins, he sat
down at the right hand of the Majesty in heaven." (Hebrews 1:3)*

Grace is the greatest free gift next to salvation, aside the greatest
earned gift of all, love. Your word is equal to your name. Your name represents your word. Your word is your character based on the decision for
others and God to trust you. Your name will always travel farther and faster
than your feet ever will! Honing your character requires being simplistic,

yet filled with wisdom, common sense and highly vulnerable to those who are your sincere friends. Imperative is for you to understand that everyone is born with unique talents, gifts, treasures. Their personalities and character traits are linked to their Genetic Code (GC) and Distinguishing Notable Attributes (DNA). *"Out of his fullness we have all received grace in place of grace already given." (John 1:16)*

Your Genetic Code is formed from within. Your spirit, personality, thought process, likes and dislikes, and actions explain why you are the way you are. Your way of life should define your capacity and distinguish your differences. Your DNA defines your external capabilities; your talents, gifts, abilities and willingness to lead or follow. Your history is relative to how you live. Having a vision, couple with wisdom, knowledge and a plan will determine your future. Realize, however, your perfect plans are awesome, if you don't have a problem with God exercising His Sovereign authority to change them to His plans. Making plans are great and a must, for plans equate to knowledge and vision for wise actions, which lend to highly likely successes. Without both, we fall short and perish for lack thereof. *"My people are destroyed from lack of knowledge. Because you have rejected knowledge." (Hosea 4:6)*

Make sound plans for today in preparation for tomorrow. Do not make plans based on tomorrow, for today has its own challenges and needs to be met. What is critically important is that your plans are in the center of God's Will, through prayer and meditating on His Word with your well laid plans. The Source tells us to ask Him for anything in our hearts and it will be done. That is from a pure heart and your heart's desires are for your best interest and upbuilding the Kingdom of the Creator. *"Therefore, do not worry about tomorrow, for tomorrow will worry about itself. Each day has enough trouble of its own." (Matthew 6:34)* Life is always better if you focus on your current needs first, then plan for tomorrow's needs as means are available and to do better. Scripture informs us and instructs us on both these precepts of enlightenment for our well-being and to help us focus on the priorities.

To make right decisions, you must be true to a higher standard and higher understanding to which you belong. Each day should be started with you seeking a sacred relationship with the Sovereign power Jesus Christ. Christ desires to be your first love, the center of your life, and your only source. He created you for a covenant relationship and in Him you are able to live in the fullness of life. This fullness of life is through His unselfish divine actions, gaining permission from God to be a sacrifice and gift unto Him. He desires to redeem all of His people back to Him, as His own. This required Jesus to leave His heavenly home and give up sitting at the right hand of God in His deity. He became lowly as man, to serve humanity. He accepted His Father's condition to be willing to suffer horrifically and bear all sins – past, present and future. He was willing to be crucified and embrace death, only to be buried to rise again and ascend back to His deity status. These acts of individual servitude and ultimate sacrifice produced His grace so that you would be free to have life without wrath on earth and life eternal after your earthly death. Death is not to be feared, for in His grace, by His defeat of death, you will die and have a better life, which is the path to return home to be with the Lord in heaven.

Grace is a part of Christ deity. You are a part of His Sovereign Will, inheriting the fullness of His power and promises by His Word. His Word is everlasting and cannot be broken by Himself or the Father. Christ committed to loving you first and making a covenant with you. This covenant is to never end, and you are to be with Him in Paradise when you leave your physical body and transcend in your spiritual body. *"Now I commit you to God and to the word of his grace, which can build you up and give you an inheritance among all those who are sanctified." (Acts 20:32)* He knows you by name. He designed your DNA and laid out your Genetic Code down to the number of hairs on your head and your unique and different personality. You were made a little less perfect than the angels but, in His image, and likeness. His Word is all and everlasting for you to have faith in Him and for your word to be of the highest standard.

Your word is equal to your name. Your name represents your word and character based on the ability for others and God to trust you. Honing your character requires being simplistic, yet filled with wisdom, common sense and highly vulnerable to those who are your friends. Be filled with the Spirit of God and immersed in His Word, holiness and wisdom. Like Christ, have compassion for people, with agape love and as needed, tough love.

Your Genetic Code and DNA are accompanied by education, employment, cultures, environment, role models and experiences related to your history and present day for affecting tomorrow and your future. You must not let the winds of life toss you from thought to thought, place to place or person to person, like the tempest of the winds. You must be steadfast in your path and journey, knowing your true identity and to whom you belong. Identify which way the winds are blowing in your life so that Christ may direct your path and journey for what He has in store for you to do. Be equipped for the journey. Do not go empty handed, only depart after the Creator has equipped you with His provisions. You must change paths as Christ speaks to you and turns your way to a better path and azimuth. There are soft winds and calm seas in the presence of God where peaceful living does exist and you can thrive. *"When the south wind blew softly, supposing that they had obtained their desire putting out to sea, they sailed close by Crete." (Acts 27:13)*

Perfecting your character through grace is to make the right decisions most of the time. You are imperfect to make the best decisions all the time. But, by grace, you are able to make simple the complexity of life. *"But by the grace of God I am what I am, and his grace to me was not without effect. No, I worked harder than all of them--yet not I, but the grace of God that was with me." (1 Corinthians 15:10)* Knowing your spiritual bearings, capacity and capability for each moment of life gives strength to your 'now' faith of your journey along the path. And it prepares and girds your confidence and courage for the numerous destinations to embark upon towards your final destiny. As you mature and grow in your relationship with Jesus Christ, you can rely on your confidence and salient gut check to be certain that your first choice will be right in grace 95% of the time. The remaining 5% of tough decisions and choices should seek grace first and patience secondly for God to change the things you cannot.

You should seek sage advice, wisdom, knowledge and prayer through great faith in the Lord and measured confidence within your small circle of proven yin and yang family, friends and advisors. However, to forget grace and ignore knowledge, wisdom and understanding is to embrace selfishness and foolishness for advice. In time, you will find yourself setting gaze on the ripples of pain, frustration, failure and defeat by everyone else who created the storms on the waters of life. You must own your decision and outcomes, otherwise, time and tests will prove you to be deemed a fool. You are a peculiar and special person and wonderfully created. You were made in the image of God and His likeness to take responsibility and accountability for all things under your authority and to endure to give the Source thanks for His grace.

In grace, you can forgive as Christ forgave and continues to forgive you to be free to live and not be shackled to the bondage of despair. You do not have to be chained to imperfect acts and decisions for a life sentence from a mistake. You can be freed from being imprisoned in your own mind's heavy emotional toll, due to a sin and without purpose of life. *"Grace to all who love our Lord Jesus Christ with an undying love." (Ephesians 6:24)* Forgiveness is the doorway to freedom to love and live as imperfect people, without feeling less than others through forgiving self and others. You must still abhor the sin and act of hurt, deceit, and betrayal by another. You are never required to forget, but to release both self and the person to strive to live peaceably. Only Jesus can give full forgiveness, as only He can judge and pass judgment. Just as only He can work through you to perform miracles in situations that does not make sense and resolve matters decades old.

You should not live the full life of King Solomon who participated and lived in sin for sensual pleasures, happiness, power, the love of riches and abounding material things. He loved power, riches, control and sex, yet he was considered the greatest king on earth and loved God. It was all a glass ceiling bubble that burst, for he found that all of his accumulations, accolades and women [over 1,000 wives and concubines] left him with an empty heart and a spirit void of a true spiritual relationship with the Source and the Vine. He had the promise through the Davidic covenant of His father, but in that he asked God for wisdom and wealth was also granted to him. He deceived himself that He had everything, but it was all vanity without the perfect relationship of grace, love and the touch of Jesus Christ. Whatsoever Solomon's eyes gazed upon and desired, it stayed not away from him. The contrast is that he was the richest and wisest man that ever lived and came from a great family lineage. He knew of the Creator through his father David and grandfather Jessie. Perhaps he did not fully understand His journey and destiny. Certainly, he was well taught in core values and in the knowledge of the Lord through his father David, and his mother Bathsheba who was familiar with pain, grief, loss, dysfunction, and a sense of betrayal by King David towards God. David had blood on his hands, which came at a great personal loss. It was the consequence and cost of sinning against God, at a price he was unwilling to pay – the death of their first son. David later accepted the death of his son and fully rejoiced that God was still great and Sovereign. Yet, Christ, the unblemished Son of God, was without sin! *"How much more, then, will the blood of Christ, who through the eternal Spirit offered himself unblemished to God, cleanse our*

consciences from acts that lead to death, so that we may serve the living God!"
(Hebrews 9:14)

God is true to His Word and not even those who chase after His heart shall be exempted for being disobedient to His Word. In this case, it meant death would come early, eight years later of the illegitimate child between David and Bathsheba in their adulterous sin. After all, her adulterer David had his most loyal friend and spiritual senior military commander Uriah sent into the front of battle to be killed. In order to protect David's sin and shame of betrayal by making his friend's wife pregnant with his child, the loss of trust and honor was shame. And, by robbing Uriah's wife of her love and loyalty to her husband came with much suffering and loss to her family. The king entrapped her. She either submitted to his sexual demand or potentially risked being killed to prevent her from telling Uriah that his best friend and king demanded sexual relations from her. Bathsheba did become the king's wife much later, after becoming pregnant by David pursuing her in adultery, while Uriah was leading the king's men in victories over King David's enemies. It is critical to gain trust, but more important to honor this trust with those who have given you theirs and received yours. The greatest trust rests in the Source, who is spirit and truth! Christ is the trust factor of God and only through Him can we have trust and faithfulness for forgiveness and an eternal life. Only through our trust in Him for grace, salvation and repentance can come mercy and a pardon of our sins.

The son who was born out of adultery died. Bathsheba cried as David prayed and fasted for days for the Lord to show mercy, but God could not become a liar to His Word. Through mercy and grace, founded on unconditional love, David was given a second chance, and Bathsheba was blessed to give birth to the seed Solomon that would bear the lineage of Abraham to bring forth the family lineage for the Savior of the world. How great is God's grace to forgive and even hide our sins from His face and Christ's, forever erasing them and requiring that we not live in sin anymore. *"I tell you, use worldly wealth to gain friends for yourselves, so that when it is gone, you will be welcomed into eternal dwellings. Whoever can be trusted with very little can also be trusted with much, and whoever is dishonest with very little will also be dishonest with much. So if you have not been trustworthy in handling worldly wealth, who will trust you with true riches?" (Luke 16:9-11)*

The essential point of sharing this story is to let you know that you have the capacity in the mind to do carnal things never considered. If your mind and soul is not responsible to a higher authority, you will become a sharer of poor character with Satan to shock family and friends. Deceit will cause family and friends to question how you could stoop so low in character and violate God's grace. But, Solomon, like His father David, did good and righteous before the Lord, chasing after His heart, to find favor in His eyes. However, how dangerous and how profoundly stupid is it to risk destroying the relationship with Christ and be abandoned on earth and denied entrance into heaven? Specifically, if a man or woman become lonely and isolated, emotional desires for lust and greed build and lead to ruin and out of God's grace. Great character and human worth require you to live by a set of principles and core values. These tenants form the lodestone in your soul, heart and spirit to direct you during the challenges you will face. This behavior leads to the grace you will be under to find favor and forgiveness in the Lord, to achieve greatness. This character of a person does not take exception, but, is heightened in character spiritually if you fear the Lord in both reverence and wrath, which is the beginning of wisdom and discipline.

When you submit to the Source, you gain a good measure of understanding and the declaration daring to not become one who violates His commandments. If you do, you could risk loss of all possessions, family and even your life. If you are true in character spiritually and on one accord in Christ, you will embrace and yearn to worship God continually and praise

Him and the Son. Your heart and soul will endure to be in the preciousness of His grace, mercy and favor.

I have reached the verdict that the essence of life in *the art of living well* reaches a conclusion of the whole matter to simply do what is right. There is where you will find joy and relevance to your life. Solomon and me, conclude that the truth of Jesus Christ is in building a personal and spiritual growing relationship with God. In living abundantly, you must recognize and work diligently to foster and command your character to be honorable, righteous, obedient, faithful, and holy. Be holy as the Source is Holy, for these are the ingredients for a great soul, and pleasing spirit, which the Lord can use as His special agent and ambassador on earth.

Weigh your life down with the Word of the Lord and the Holy Spirit to fight spiritually by putting on the full armor of God. You are to dawn the helmet of salvation, belt of truth, breastplate of righteousness, sandals of peace, sword of power (His Word) and the shield of faith. The armor of God will protect you from fiery darts and piercing tongues from people who does not know Christ or the art of living. *"Put on the full armor of God, so that you can take your stand against the devil's schemes." (Ephesians 6:11)* Keep your azimuth pointed along the path of God's Will in your journey. Do not lose your lodestone, the Holy Spirit, which will help you to focus on God's will, not your will. Be above reproof, so that your name rings with a great melody when mentioned to others.

The lodestone was created by God and discovered by man to point towards the North Star, the Star of David and Bright Morning Star. The lodestone can only be found in six places on earth to build compasses to navigate ships and terrain. There is a spiritual lodestone, the Holy Spirit that Christ gives to all who believes in Him and God the Father. *"I, Jesus, have sent my angel to give you this testimony for the churches. I am the Root and the Offspring of David, and the bright Morning Star." (Revelation 22:16)*

The Holy Spirit is given to the body of the church to guide your thoughts and ways during the Christian journey of *the art of living*. He will turn your mind and heart northward to Jesus Christ in all situations and conditions if your Genetic Code and DNA spirit is submissive to the Holy Spirit by free will choice. The Holy Spirit is an extension of Christ from the Father to indwell within you, always turning your mind, heart, spirit and soul northward to Jesus Christ, His righteousness and love. Regardless of your individual situation, if the spirit that encompasses your Genetic Code and DNA is submissive to the Holy Spirit by free will choice, you are connected to the Source, Jesus Christ and your petitions go before God with promises. Surely, the opposite of this action will cause negative reactions and consequences, not just for you, but also for all who depend on you and love you. *"The Holy Spirit was showing by this that the way into the Most Holy Place had not yet been disclosed as long as the first tabernacle was still functioning." (Hebrews 9:8)*

Your selfish perspective without enlightenment will lead to a great demise and grave limitations and grief which will not be quick or easy to handle or endure. However, there is none greater in faithfulness, grace and mercy than the Source who is divine and sovereign – Jesus the Christ. All of these attributes are supernatural for Jesus, which you can have if you give your life to Christ through belief, repentance and a contrite spirit. You would do well to allow Him to have total control of your life through His Spirit. You must come into the enlightenment that the Source inhabits and holds the highest righteousness, and that all of His works are splendid and majestic, to endure forever. *"For this very reason, make every effort to add to your faith with goodness; and to goodness, knowledge, and to knowledge self-control; and to self-control, perseverance; and to perseverance, godliness; and to godliness, mutual from being ineffective and unproductive in you r knowledge of our Lord Jesus Christ." (2 Peter 1:5-8)*

"My son, do not forget my teaching, but keep my commands in your heart, for they will prolong your life many years and bring you peace and prosperity. Let love and faithfulness never leave you; bind them around your neck, write them on the tablet of your heart.

Then you will win favor and a good name in the sight of God and man. Trust in the LORD with all your heart and lean not on your own understanding; in all your ways submit to him, and he will make your paths straight." (Proverbs 3:1-6)

ANTIDOTE 28 |
NEVER LET A GREAT
OPPORTUNITY PASS YOU BY

"When one becomes complacent, one becomes comfortable
and dependable on that which they already know and have, and
their great opportunities remain oblivious!" Erogies Grigley Jr.

Does life seem to hand you one difficult day after another, filled with pain, grief, sorrow and hardship? Consider the reasons for your weariness and tests that seem never ending. Your difficulties are not where you are headed but rather what you will soon put in your past. God may possibly be trying to get your attention in testing you for a wonderful opportunity. Once He has your heart and mind, He can lead your spirit to a better place that is no longer filled with hurt, sorrow and stressful days and difficult nights. Opportunities given by the Lord can come with hard work, but nevertheless, a blessing that you can give thanks for and hold your head high. *"And pray for us, too, that God may open a door for our message, so that we may proclaim the mystery of Christ, for which I am in chains." (Colossians 4:3)*

Always avoid people who are fast talkers and offers you the world. In foresight, you are strongly encouraged to hang up the phone or run if this sort of person makes it to your ear or presence with such dangerous foolishness and buffoonery. Resting, ruminating and resolving the difference between Murphy's Law and The Real McCoy as an opportunity or disaster must be done quickly and decidedly, using instincts and experience, with prayer. When you apply insight, foresight, prayer, patience, knowledge, wisdom and instincts with common sense, you will never be defeated or be taken advantage of by a swindler, leech, liar or opportunist. Instead, look at the opportunity as a good thing or bad thing. If it does not quack, it is not a duck. If it does not mow, it is not a cow, regardless of its looks! Recognize people for who they are and ensure you look into inquires of their present and past lives. Look at who they associate with and who they are in relationships with before inviting a person into your circle and giving them your money, time and friends to a scheme. You must call a thing a thing for what it is! This position must be taken regardless of your emotions and the other person's emotional plea.

The art of living well is in 'I am' for opportunities of blessings and to build a legacy. Many overlook signs and wonders, and even a phone call or visit with an opportunity to change their lives forever. Many times, you see an opportunity in a challenging, fearful or unfamiliar way and fail to move out of your complacency. When you become complacent, you become both comfortable and dependent on that which you already have, and the great opportunities will pass you by. Slow your heart rate, feel your pulse and listen to the process of 'is there added value' and 'does this align with my prayers to Christ?' Most times, what appears to be confusing, does not make sense or is false. If it does not make sense with peace to your inner spirit, the opportunity cannot find agreement with your inner person. This only happens when you hear the from the Spirit and see the blessing unfold. *"Seek the LORD while he may be found; call on him while he is near." (Isaiah 55:6)*

Be attached to God, whose name is "I Am", and who is your Source. God took a portion of His divine nature, upon which He laid your soul. Then He wrapped the two into one. With your soul wrapped in His divine nature, He blew His Spirit into the creation to give you life, shaped in

His likeness. He took the three and sent you from heaven through time and space to earth to be clothed in the flesh of humanity. Once you took the first breath of fresh air, you became a living being for God's Divine and sole purpose along His path for all opportunities of righteousness. You must know that the Source and the Creator are not slack concerning their promises voiced spiritually or audibly. As some men and women look at delayed gratification and delayed blessings as a form of slackness and disappointment, they miss out on the beauty of what is to come by being patient and well doing.

Honorable and anointed men and women are apt to believe and reason that God sets an appointed time. Time is very important, and appointments should be met with zeal. Being true to value time is in direct spiritual contrast to a person's carnal walk, who constantly changes their appointment time. Or, you are always late or miss the appointment due to a lack of character and respect. But there is an appointment that everyone will be punctual to attend – death. *"And it is appointed to men once to die, but after this the judgment." (Hebrews 9:27)* Opportunities of grace and mercy are from God which He gives as gifts and favor to create opportunities, under His Will. You should recognize that the Lord is Sovereign, He reigns in grace to be longsuffering to His children, to ensure each one lives an abundant and joyful life. Even in the midst of overwhelming challenges, all can make heaven their destiny with expectations of great success. *"Be very careful, then, how you live--not as unwise but as wise, making the most of every opportunity, because the days are evil. Therefore, do not be foolish, but understand what the Lord's will is." (Ephesians 5:15-17)*

God will continue to truly remain in Deity and Sovereignty. He is long-suffering in His faithfulness. Thereby giving His people more time for the blessed opportunity to grow into a progressive relationship with Him and Jesus Christ, as a mature and faithful believer.

When you are in the Will of God, His favor is for those with great faith, but sometimes may fall. Our discipline should be to remain obedient and be content with His grace and mercy. He desires for you to be His legacy on earth, just and righteous, as managers of the earth and as loving neighbors with one another. When you are patient, you become the very focus of His Divine blossoms of spirit, truth, giving, serving and loving – the true legacies. He planned for your legacy to be prosperous and a to have a long life and to pass the legacy of blessings on to each of your children, little by little. These blossoms bear the divine opportunities in fruits of love, joy, peace, faith, hope, kindness and fulfilling, to uplift others and glorify God the Father, Jesus Christ the Son and the Holy Spirit!

When you earn income for a living, the financial legacy for an inheritance begins with returning a bountiful and cheerful portion back to the Source for the church and the Kingdom, allowing you to keep up to 90% of your first fruit income. The fruits are what you receive, not what you would have received. The church is a hospital and orphanage, for the lost, sick, poor, hurting, wayward and downtrodden. The Scripture of Christ separating heavenly from earthly perspectives is well known by mature Christians. When Jesus was challenged, and an attempt was made by spies to trick Him regarding His deity and responsibility to lawfully pay taxes, Christ asked whose image and inscription was on the denarius coin? Then Christ said, *"Render therefore to Caesar the things which are Caesar and render unto God that which is God's." (Luke 20:25)* God requires you to pay taxes to the government that are due. He who is, was and are, also commands you to give to God a portion of what He has blessed you with for your home, to go into His storehouse. He requires you to give a generous portion back to Him from your finances, gifts, talents, and treasures. *"Give generously to them and do so without a grudging heart; then because of this the LORD your God will bless you in all your work and in everything you put your hand to." (Deuteronomy 15:10)*

This act of obedience is done out of reverence and discipline, through love, faith, thankfulness and gratefulness for what He has done and does for you and your home. He should not have to command such, but He did! To dishonor this requirement is to deny your legacy being intact, let alone your daily life that seems to always be just above water, a few inches from drowning in debt, frustration, losses, envy, jealousy and lack of quality of life. For your condition to change in mind, heart and spirit, your attitude must change, and your behavior must shift to stop the bad behavior of being at odds and out of alignment with the Lord. You ought to live to please the Lord and find tender new mercies, unspeakable joy and unsurpassing peace at every sunrise and at each sunset.

After you make your mind, heart and spirit right with the Lord, you should make it right with your tithes and offering. Then you should build your emergency savings (one year of income or greater), retirement planning, children's college fund and a nest egg of investments which will allow for living abundantly during life, your living years and elderly years. With this financial guidance, you should want to leave an inheritance for your children, and for their children. The most important inheritance to leave as a legacy is to impart the Word of the Lord into your children, on doors, bedposts and in their hearts. This is your legacy to live in Christ, and He will sup with you in a growing relationship for you to pass the blessing to the heads of each of your children – for Christ and your children are your legacies! Well done good and faithful, honorable and noble servant, friend and adopted family member. The Kingdom of God should be your aim, passed on by your actions, prayer life and walk with Christ. Leave a legacy as a good person and an inheritance pleasing to the Lord! *Each of you should give what you have decided in your heart to give, not reluctantly or under compulsion, for God loves a cheerful giver." (2 Corinthians 9:7)*

There are tremendous opportunities in serving the Lord, where He will pour out immeasurable blessings on the just and righteous, which are beyond material and financial. Honor the Lord and know that where you are isn't your destiny or your final chapter. The Lord has already prospered over your future and the life you will live. He has purposed to give you a life of prosperity and longevity.

"This is what the Sovereign LORD says: If the prince makes a gift from his inheritance to one of his sons, it will also belong to his descendants; it is to be their property by inheritance." (Ezekiel 46:16)

ANTIDOTE 29 |
FIND PEACE IN YES
AND JOY IN NO

*"True love does not make choices with consideration or compassion
for the other love. Neither does tough love wrestle with truth, right
and fairness, to either say yes or no!" Erogies Grigley Jr.*

Have you experienced times where heavy grief fell upon you? Often times
when sorrow, pain, grief and anguish visit our spirits, our hearts and minds
fall victim to 'woe is me'. Do not be alarmed or feel all alone, for you are
not the only one to experience such mental torment in feeling let down or
facing an overwhelming decision. Neither are you alone in life, for there
is a Comforter you can call and depend on. Have you experienced periods
where the Lord has been silent with you? Perhaps, you need to change your
environment or people you keep company with for the favor of the Lord to
be unveiled and your prayers answered. *"Above all, my brothers and sisters, do
not swear—not by heaven or by earth or by anything else. All you need to say is
a simple "Yes" or "No." (James 5:12)*

Everyone desires to belong; therefore, to live together requires both
agape and tough love to be embraced. Both 'yes' and 'no' are from origins
of the mind, spirit and heart, manifested in the conscious of character and
your words. Your word is equal to your name. Your name represents your
character, based on the ability for others and God to trust and respect you.

Your great desire should be focused on the Giver's peace and joy, within your being as the receiver of such grand and marvelous gifts. Often, the emotional tugging is for satisfaction, usually temporal and fleeting emotional happiness for both.

Often times, you must make the decision to say "No" to those closest to you in order to refute being an enabler. Saying "no" can free you and others from unnecessary stressors that can come from damaging situations. Sometimes, tough love must be exercised, and the wiser person must 'drop Lot', as Abraham did with his nephew Lot in Genesis 13. Notice that God had been silent with Abraham for years, but once he removed Lot from his presence and home, only then did God revisit Abraham and give him the promise made before his journey began. *"Rejoice in the Lord always. I will say it again: Rejoice! Let your gentleness be evident to all. The Lord is near. Do not be anxious about anything, but in every situation, by prayer and petition, with thanksgiving, present your request to God." (Philippians 4:4-6)*

Your thought process to resist embracing tough love towards another, to hold one responsible and accountable serves as personal, mental and emotional enablers, not spiritual as game changers and warriors. The giver and the receiver share the same desired outcome to not feel embarrassed or uncomfortable in the yes or no effect. True love does not make choices with the compassion for the other's love. Neither does tough love wrestle with truth, right and fairness to either say yes or no. You simply find the strength to ask the five salient drivers for burning answers of the mind and spirit: Why am I in this situation? What is the love for? Why ask me for the love? Will this love endure? And, am I willing to take this desire on?

The giver's decision to invoke tough love understands that "no and 'yes' are equal in transparency, yet 'no' becomes greater in spiritual peace and spiritual ownership when tough love is exercised to indirectly promote agape love and exercise your instincts. However, to everyone else desiring emotional happiness and not love, the giver becomes the denier and deemed having made a fool out of the one that received not. When you place another's needs above your own, you are deemed a fool and shall bear the consequences, which accomplishes defeating acts, stemming from desires and lusts of the flesh, along with betrayal. *"So Abram said to Lot, 'Let's not have any quarreling between you and me, or between your herders and mine, for we are close relatives. Is not the whole land before you? Let's part company. If you go to the left, I'll go to the right; if you go to the right, I'll go to the left'."* (Genesis 13:8-9)

Many people are known to subconsciously buy what they want, and after their treasures are spent, these people consciously beg for what they need. These are fools, who will repeat the chronic pattern of denial and risk until tough love and enlightenment occupy their characters, absent of death. Let your 'yes' be yes, and your 'no' be no so that you can truly experience *the art of living*! The greatest challenge to say 'no' is simply and truthfully you, and you not being bold enough to be wise and courageous to be just and righteous!

You have tendencies to live in the moment and not say 'no' to the urges that come with pride, conceit, lust and greed for self-fulfillment and material possessions. When you give into these urges to spend your hard-earned money, you become a victim to the very game that causes ruin, falling away from faith and the church, even separating from your spouse and family. Spending is a disease of the weak spirit, but not one that cannot be cured, for it is of the heart and mind. You simply have to hearken to the Word of the Lord and speak boldly against the thoughts of the evil one that tells you it is okay to buy the new thing, toy, clothing or car; some even take expensive trips on credit for which there is no cash in the bank to cover. Foolishness, pride and selfishness with greed come in like a roaring lion and overwhelms poor wisdom to become sounding brass beating in the air to create an irritable noise in your mind and a stabbing in your heart. And, if you are not careful, there will occur a great loss in hearing the voice of the Spirit from the Lord. This behavior, my friend, is dangerous and contagious!

Lastly, be mindful of family and church folks who prey on those who work hard, spend frugally and save wisely, while saying they are praying for you. They are not the ones who work smart and manage to live within their financial means. Those who have no shame or regard for respecting you will come and ask for money, because they embrace the behavior of fools and victims of the disease of being addicts to capitalism – spending money, buying stuff. To break their cycle is for you to not be an enabler to their bad behaviors and habits. Just say 'no, I don't have it to give' and mean it. If they take a hard stance with you to make you feel guilty, they really are not friends or respectful family members who want to claim your hard-earned wages as their own. Their cycle is to get paid and buy what they want and desire. Then, they find a gullible person who does not do well with challenges and who has money to feed their weakness of spending unwisely. This type of person will literally rob you through sorrowful pleas and broken promises, as you give your treasures to the passions of swine that they are. Be careful, for they will trample on your pearls—heart, mind and spirit.

Remember, love is not blind, love never fails and love is simply pure. Love does not give into greed and pride. It resists the temptation of lusts and passes the test of holding you responsible and accountable to self and the Lord for a better and nobler life, to be proud of. After all, the Scriptures record in Proverbs 37 that the Lord has never forsaken the righteous person, nor has the seed of the righteous been seen begging for bread or other means for living. If your friends and family members are truly righteous, they will not take from you or try to deceive you, as family is bound to share, help and love one another in unity and strength. Truly spiritual and faithful Christians will always choose obedience and humility while refraining from asking for or accepting handouts and bailouts. Their faith and trust are in the Lord, and their good works are with discipline, preparedness and wisdom. Family and friends should not be placed in a position to ask what they can do for you, regardless of how small or large their giving could be! *"If I give all I possess to the poor and give over my body to hardship that I may boast, but do not have love, I gain nothing. Love is patient, love is kind. It does not envy, it does not boast, it is not proud. It does not dishonor others, it is not self-seeking, it is not easily angered, it keeps no record of wrongs. Love does not delight in evil but rejoices with the truth. It always protects, always trusts, always hopes, always perseveres. Love never fails…".* (1 Corinthians 13:3-8)

Your behaviors and motives within yourself towards or against specific agape deeds are at the heart that identifies the perfect or imperfect nature of a person. What is life without love? Everyone desires to belong to someone; therefore, to live together requires both agape and tough love to be embraced with a compassion. Consider denying self and seeking your own will, for the pursuit of humility and love and watch the precious benefits and fruit unfold. Your great desire should be focused on the giver's peace and joy and being a receiver of such grand and marvelous gifts reciprocated.

Tough love does not wrestle with consideration or compassion for neither yes nor no. The giver's decision to invoke tough love, understands that 'no' and 'yes' are equal in transparency. Yet, 'no' becomes greater in spiritual peace and spiritual ownership when tough love is exercised to indirectly promote agape love. This attitude places the heart, spirit and mind on one accord. However, to everyone else desiring emotional happiness and not love, the giver becomes the denier and deemed having made a fool out of the one that received not. *"The way of fools seems right to them, but the wise listen to advice."* (Proverbs 12:15)

Many people are known to intentionally buy what they want, and after their monies are gone, they go to others with money and beg for helping them meet their priorities. Again, these are fools who repeat the chronic pattern of denial and risk until tough love and enlightenment occupy their character. When the giant of your life stumbles or falls from your blow, take not your weapon to kill such a thing, but take their very own weapon and annihilate the enemy of your present and future, to assure others, neither yourself will fall victim. Or, you shall face them again!

There are abundant reasoning and observations for you to be joyous and at peace in life. You are to live and make simple the difficulty of turning lemons into experiencing refreshing lemonade. You can also help to turn a wayward and hardened heart into a pliable, compassionate and loving spirit. So, too, is the individual perspective and approach for two people to live together, as true and guaranteed friends. Focused on their love for higher norms to achieve the greatest harvest from their union as one and doing great works individually and collectively.

If you are attentive and take responsibility for the giants of pain, sickness, suffering, divorce, unemployed, wayward child, and death as their own, they create the atmosphere for the positive realities that occur at their appointed times. Seek not your own will, but rather let humility and compassion for your fellow man and woman be sought as the right and perfect will. Live for the specific purpose spoken by the Lord to carry His authority and promise into manifestation in the lives of those who are truly in need.

The sun rises and sets over the earth, but the sun never asks a favor or promise from Mother Nature or humanity for the rising and setting. Trees and plants are thriving in backdrop green and varied light and brilliant colors, nubs are attached, blossoms are in bloom, and fruit are harvested, void of the capacity and capability to ask the harvester for anything. People are strange and many are self-centered and all about 'what's in it for me?' This person is a leech, because they have an attitude of getting what they can. Never do they ask what can I do to simply help someone else and expect nothing in return? Rather, the positive outcome is to mature into a better and wholesome person, which should be everyone's aim.

The harvester knows by observation, wisdom, practice, and experiences over time that trees and plants require sunlight for strength and growth, and bees and butterflies for initiating the transformation and creation of blossoms and fruit. The harvester knows that these realities must be nurtured and watered. Loving is an act that promotes giving and humility, and this compassion creates greater opportunities for success than passions and personalities. Some growths are so rapid and broad that pruning is required of the trees and plants. As is in the lives of people, a friend, a mother or father, a Christian should take great pleasure in bringing hope, peace, joy and help to the least one in need, as you prune bountiful blessings to be shared with others in need.

There is a formidable giant that you have to face in order to move into your purpose and receive the rewards of His promise. These giants are challenges on the mountain, down in the valley, highs and lows, and in your spiritual walk, as tests and trials rise in your life. They are influenced by another to demand a blessing in advance, before this person even prays for one. This person must receive a touch and call from Jesus to meet them as they are in their imperfect and divisive behavior in order for you to have the opportunity to help them. Wayward people require shifting of their principles, so that the old will not be removed, resisting embracing a transformation and ascension to a higher level in life. This revelation and breakthrough in spirit and heart is for the Will of the Lord to be done in them and through them for their fellow brother and sister, regardless of their state or plight.

When Jesus forgives and gives you His grace and power, it is impossible to have this experience and bestowed authority, and go backwards to a hardened, selfish and cold-hearted life. As is in Mother Nature, so too is the critical need for worrisome things to be shed in order to find and have hope, faith, joy and peace, with the fullness of liberties. All who love nature and creating things, take great joy in life to be responsible for sowing, planting, watering and nurturing. These same deeds are necessary for humankind to do well and to glorify the Lord before the harvest. *"May the God of hope fill you with all joy and peace as you trust in him, so that you may overflow with hope by the power of the Holy Spirit." (Romans 15:13)*

Understand and seek the Lord in faith and repentance to know that the Creator's and the Source's ways and thoughts are not like our minds and ways. The Lord even encourages us to have His mind and to take on lifestyles of His ways and in His likeness, for this is pleasing unto Him. Thereby, embrace that there is great joy in life in making simple the difficult and complex challenges of living. Do not get weary when facing the giants in your life. Be strong and courageous in the Source. Do not faint. Do not become overwhelmed when a giant tries to block the path to your opportunities and destiny. As a storm or tornado that comes your way, or the threat of pestilence and attacks to your family are oncoming, remember that God is in control. Because the Lord is in control and takes great pleasure in loving you, you can be assured as a righteous person striving to live in His Word and to live the gospel in your life, you will experience victory and a great hope for tomorrow. But, without the courage and will to face and fight the giant in your path, there will be no reward to be received by you. Instead, the giant will have created another victim and thwarted attacks from other potential giant slayers. The victory is the Lord's, and you must put on the whole armor of God and embrace warring with the giant blocking your path to your purpose and destiny.

Through studying and gaining knowledge and wisdom, getting the facts and truth that comes with understanding, you are increased in boldness and courage to be free to face the giants and the storms. Face them courageously as David did with the Philistine Goliath, with a rag and five smooth stones and in the Lord's strength, he fought with authority and power of Omnipotence and Omnipresence. God can create a courageous servant out of your weakness, giving you joy and peace, with a hope and promise for eternal liberties. Just in case there are giant's brothers and cousins, you are at peace for you have already destroyed the first giant singe-handily in the Lord. You still have stones of spiritual power in your arsenal to thwart the enemy of fear and robbery which are principalities of darkness in the spirit. *"The hearts of the wise make their mouths prudent, and their lips promote instruction. Gracious words are a honeycomb, sweet to the soul and healing to the bones." (Proverbs 16:23-24)*

The Lord offers promises and victories as He fills the hearts of those who seek and know Him. He imparts His precepts and anointing for you to manage and cultivate the earth and the fullness therein. Christ desires to dwell and exist within you for you to do His Will and freely take care of His works as your own. You must go through copulation in marriage for the opportunity to create the beginnings of life to be birthed through pains of childbearing labors, infant and child nurturing which are the reasoning and only supernatural way and means to reach manhood and womanhood for the continuation of sustaining life.

The Source said to take on His yoke, because His yoke is easy (filled with grace, mercy, faithfulness and power to His children) and His burden is light. (Matthew 11:30) If you find what wayward people are doing is frustrating and simplicity cannot be achieved, evict them out of your life. If not, you will face this giant of difficulty without a counter destroying strategy, as your ego and motives places you at an impasse to find peace.

Now is the time to ask for help and cast everything to the Lord, the good and the bad, for He can handle it all and make the difficult simple in brevity and actions. The Lord is on your side for those that keep the faith, live nobly and are taking in breaths of the air He created, in heaven and on earth, to do His Will and works. You must stay the course for life and face every giant and every fear that stands between you and your great opportunity. Defeat the enemy as you are dressed in the full armor of God, using the very weapons meant for victory on the evil one. Then you can shout with joy as the giant falls, given into one's hands supernaturally by the Lord.

The Source with the Holy Spirit is the teacher of truth and the bearer of good news which remains constant throughout life and the earth. Note that those who have the greatest devotional life are subject to the greater experiences, storms and challenges from many giants, but you are one who will not despair for the Lord is on your side. Never let your faith go into doubt and your character be questioned in the hours of darkness, for you are the light in Christ. You are the trusted in the faithfulness of God, as you are too powerful in Jesus to be afraid and doubt. In your time of need, the Source has already predestined all creations to be available to His believers and favored people with provisions and protection. Being of righteousness, you are there in the Lord's spiritual engagement where you can breathe and speak with boldness and dominion authority to have the fulfillment of life in *the art of living well.*

"The law of the LORD is perfect, refreshing the soul. The statutes of the LORD are trustworthy, making wise the simple. The precepts of the LORD are right, giving joy to the heart. The commands of the LORD are radiant, giving light to the eyes. The fear of the LORD is pure, enduring forever. The decrees of the LORD are firm, and all of them are righteous." (Psalm 19:7-9)

ANTIDOTE 30 |
LOVE YOURSELF. LOVE OTHERS.
GLORIFY GOD.

"You can only belong to someone else, if you are willing to give you away first." Erogies Grigley Jr.

What is life without someone to love and someone to receive love from? One of the greatest benefits of being certain of who you are is your identity in a relationship with the Lord Jesus Christ and God the Father. This love and relationship come with respect of husband and wife, and favor with parents, family and friends. Who makes you more acceptable as being an honorable person, when your name precedes your position and in conversations? When you see the love affair of the heart that you have opened, go through it. And, when the knock is at your heart's door, open it to the true love that takes your breath away. *"Love the Lord your God with all your heart and with all your soul and with all your mind and with all your strength." (Mark 12:30)*

Your versatility to live in the light of the Messiah and travel through darkness without fear and with great faith, permeates the world and liberates you as being extraordinary. This is exactly the righteous character, traits and temperament the Son of God embraces and favors: to clothe you in His glorious anointing. *"For he chose us in him before the creation of the world to be holy and blameless in his sight. In love, he predestined us for adoption to sonship through Jesus Christ, in accordance with his pleasure and will-- to the praise of his glorious grace, which he has freely given us in the One he loves." (Ephesians 1:4-6)*

Being selfish intentionally, willfully and with thoughtlessly centered motives are the first thorns to get caught in your heart. The thorn pricks rise from your pride and carnal curiosity to entertain an unfamiliar voice (evil) and unseen face (Satan). These are the same circumstances that befell man and woman in the Garden of Eden as recorded in the Scriptures. In this moment, all Adam had to do was to call on the Lord for help after hearing the unfamiliar voice with an unseen face. The failure to exercise his spiritual power and dominion authority in the Garden created a problem for all of humanity throughout all the ages to come. In one moment, with just one cry for help to the Lord, Adam could have saved himself and his wife, Eve, from eviction and the horrific anguish, losses and difficulties they endured and would later suffer for all of their days. No one loved Adam greater than his Father, God the Creator, whom He created in His own likeness and image. He even spent the cool of the evening every day with Adam, whom He was so pleased with.

Today, you also experience difficulties from not rooting out unfamiliar voices and unseen faces which attempt to place thoughts of curiosity in your mind and draw you away from your path and the beautiful *art of living well* journey God has already given you. We look at Adam, whose being was created with delicate and precision spiritual workmanship for the primary purpose of having a personal relationship with the Source and Creator. God also desired to have a personal relation between man in what seemed no imperfections. The Source was the provider and protector of the Garden of Eden where Adam dwelled alone, until God said it was not good for man to be alone. Therefore, He gave Adam a glorious and wonderful wife created from the first spiritual surgery involving a removal of a rib without using anesthetics. Because this woman was bone of Adam's bone and flesh of his flesh, they knew the kindred relationship with each other and their love for God. Do you have a kindred relationship with your husband or wife with a friendship and covenant rooted in the Lord or rooted in an unfamiliar voice and unseen face? *"Whoever dwells in the shelter of the Most High will rest in the shadow of the Almighty. I will say of the Lord, "He is my refuge and my fortress, my God, in whom I trust." Surely, he will save you from the fowler's snare and from the deadly pestilence. He will cover you with his feathers, and under his wings you will find refuge; his faithfulness will be your shield and rampart."* (Psalm 91:1-4)

Adam and Eve were living the glorious life filled with dominion authority over everything in the Garden of Eden as they were the only human beings. Even the angels worked for Adam to help cultivate and manage the Garden. This supernatural, heavenly and spiritual experience is applicable to you today if you were to slow your pace of life. Often, you can catch glimpses of angels in your life, even have visits from angels, as you behold the grace and handiwork of the Source and Creator. Joy and serenity do not last when disobedience and the blatant act of defiance enters life, by being curious about the world. Another example of this is when Lot's wife looked back at the city, when God said not to look back after He had delivered them from Sodom and Gomorrah. (Genesis 29:17) Even when God gives you specific instructions and the consequences of failing to adhere, He can still administer mercy with judgment.

The desires of the flesh and infiltration of the mind with curiosity outside of the Will of God brings in the worldly perspectives. Involving entertaining betrayal and constituting ungratefulness with the Creator and the Source. You should be humble and trust in the Lord, to whom all things are from and to whom all honor and glory must be given. Selfishness, pride, betrayal and disobedience are the negative cognitive and spiritually manifested ingredients that guarantee separation from the love of God the Father and Lord the Son. These defiant acts create consequences in the very moment you entertain carnal thoughts. When you act on these thoughts, the sadness is that you will go through trials and tribulations until there is absolute validation of a broken heart and a contrite spirit... repentance. *"Godly sorrow brings repentance that leads to salvation and leaves no regret, but worldly sorrow brings death." (2 Corinthians 7:10)*

The unfavorable acts of sin are freely committed, by the one exercising free will choice to violate the unique and honored relationship established by the Creator with His creation. This deplorable and regretful decision by Adam and Eve, and by you, occurs in the sight of God and is revealed to others who are known and unknown by the blinded one. There is hope and a remedy which exceeds and precedes the law if you know how to access such power.

Beloved, in the human experience you cannot ignore or create additions to the Sovereign Will of God. The covenant and promises God made with Abraham remained with his descendants and applies to you today. Many times, you are caught up and believe that the Will of God does not apply to you, even when His purpose is revealed to you. You must understand the purpose is not for you to benefit from but rather is for His people and the community of God. *"May our Lord Jesus Christ himself and God our Father, who loved us and by his grace gave us eternal encouragement and good hope, encourage your hearts and strengthen you in every good deed and word." (2 Thessalonians 2:16)*

So, too, is His Will for you. It is in Christ and through Christ that you are His natural descendant and adopted into the family of Christ as a part of the body of Christ as a believer and child of God. You must be obedient and discipline, chasing after God's heart and His righteousness with great faith. For this is pleasing unto the Lord!

Therefore, the law given to Adam and Eve has passed away to not eat of the fruit of knowledge of good and evil, for through their sins we were all born into a world filled with evil. However, the Law, which was given hundreds of years later to Adam's descendant never invalidated the first previous agreement of God with the Son to have a relationship with His creation humanity. Rather, the promise was made in Christ who is fulfilling the inheritance of the promise of God that is not dependent on the Law. The relationship is out of the grace of God and through His Beloved Son Jesus Christ. Jesus is who God graciously gave us through Abraham who was there from the beginning, with blessings and a promise, which you are the inheritor. Because humanity's imperfections will lead to offenses that are not pleasing unto the Source and Creator, the Law was given for governance and to deter sin. The Scripture established obedience amongst God's chosen people and charged you to be submissive to the Word of the Lord, which is right before God.

Because of love, unconditionally tried and true, God made it possible for love to conquer all and cover a multitude of sins and heathenism. *"He brought me out into a spacious place; he rescued me because he delighted in me." (2 Samuel 22:20)* The Source, Jesus Christ, had to come through thousands of years of time and trillions of miles of space to fulfill the first blessings of the promise made with Abraham. Christ alone is the author of better promises with God's full power and authority and supersedes the Law and the first covenant. Thereby, making these covenants obsolete as Jesus is the new covenant, founded on better promises. God made man and woman a little lower than the angels, and Christ stepped down from His deity and was made a little lower than the angels to take on human form to experience the fullness of humanities' weaknesses, pains and challenges, yet without sin through a virgin. His perfect spiritual nature was not carnal in nature. Rather in divinity for the ultimate purpose of His human life of 33 years to become a perfect sacrifice to endure suffering, crucifixion, and death. His death allowed for God's resurrection of His beloved Son, enabling God to bestow Christ as the better promises with a covenant. Jesus was given all authority and power over heaven and earth as the Mediator of a better covenant, founded on better promises.

Now through the Source as the Mediator, no longer do you not have an Intercessor, but the Source and the Holy Spirit are interceding and praying for you before God. Righteousness and grace are the ingredients to manifest the new relationship for you with Christ through repentance of heart and spirit, contrite for pleasing and honoring the Father, Son, and Holy Spirit. Because of His holiness and righteousness as the Mediator for all of humanity that believes in Him, unlike the Law, He gives life and restores righteousness in you. He alone locked up all things under sin, became sin Himself without sinning and defeated Satan to take the sting out of death, so that in your belief and faithfulness in the deity of Jesus Christ, abundant and eternal life is given to you.

Through Christ, you can enjoy life, love yourself, and love your family and friends. You the believer receives all the benefits of grace and mercy, along with rewards from Christ and God the Father. You can live again, enjoy life again, to love yourself, love family, love others and love the Source. As He glorifies God the Father for your future, to prosper you in your journey, along the path of *the art of living*, which will take you to your destiny in the Spirit. *"Even to your old age and gray hairs I am he, I am he who will sustain you. I have made you and I will carry you; I will sustain you and I will rescue you." (Isaiah 46:4)*

Being loved by others starts with loving and respecting self. It is a necessity to respect and value yourself and have means to take care of yourself, family and the Lord's charge to the church. Then you can live in the Will of Christ and be equipped to have compassion for helping others. It is under Christ's wings of protection and the infilling of His Spirit that fills you spiritually with heavenly knowledge, wisdom and understanding, which produces humility, love and selflessness to do great works. These tenants are to help you and your fellow man rise from within your core foundation – your soul. Build your life on being Christlike, to be the manager and caretaker for all things, small and great, that God entrusts you with. *"For Christ's love compels us, because we are convinced that one died for all, and therefore all died." (2 Corinthians 5:14)*

Trust, faithfulness and favor is not for one, but for all whose purpose is in the Will of Christ. We should live to please Christ and glorify God for the sole purpose of tending to His people and creations for salvation and life eternal. You belong to Jesus Christ, therefore in His glory are your blessings and favor on earth. This favor comes from your great 'now' faith, coupled with good deeds and sincere works, which will give you a glorious crown as one of your heavenly rewards. You are an heir to the Kingdom and according to the promises of Jesus Christ, you who have been sanctified, justified, and glorified to enter into Paradise. There you will know the fullness of His glory and unconditional love, as your name is sealed in the Lambs Book of Life.

"May our Lord Jesus Christ himself and God our Father,
who loved us and by his grace gave us eternal encouragement
and good hope, encourage your hearts and strengthen you in every good deed
and word." (2 Thessalonians 2:16)

ANTIDOTE 31 |
MAKE THE DIFFICULTY
OF LIVING SIMPLE

*"There comes a time in life when you must rise
above your difficulties." Erogies Grigley Jr.*

Have you been facing difficult times? Does the attitude of fear creep in? Have you thought about quitting or giving up? This attitude is unhealthy and prevents you from pursuing your purpose in life. Know that you are not alone and there is a resolution to your challenges in life. *"Be careful for nothing; but in everything by prayer and supplication with thanksgiving let your requests be made known to God." (Philippians 4:6)*

In life, you must come into an enlightenment to live and make simple the difficulty of living in a world sick and hurting. So, too, is the individual perspective and approach for two people to live together, as true and guaranteed that their love will last. Living in honor, faith and discipline are heavenly principles to achieve the greatest harvest from your union and great works, individually and together. If you are attentive to your love, there are realities that occur at appointed times. This love seeks only to do the Will of the Creator, for the specific purpose spoken unto the reality of living to love and loving to live.

The sun rises and sets over the earth by the hand of God. Mother Nature and humanity are the Lord's footstool and precious creation. The harvester knows that the realities of sowing and watering seeds must be nurtured for plants to grow, as a lover must know the same in their love affair of the heart, spirit and soul for their true love. Loving is an act that far exceeds giving, and humility and compassion creates greater opportunity for success than passion and helping. Some growths are so rapid and broad that pruning is required of the trees and plants; as is in the lives of people – selfishness, ego, pride. Some things must be shed in order to find and have joy and peace, with the fullness of liberties. All who love nature and creating take great joy in life to be responsible for planting, watering and nurturing these awesome needs for humankind and to glorify the Lord before the harvest. *"I planted the seed, Apollos watered it, but God has been making it grow. So neither the one who plants nor the one who waters is anything, but only God, who makes things grow." (1 Corinthians 3:6-7)*

You must understand and seek the Lord in faith and repentance to know that the Creator and the Source's ways and thoughts are not like our minds and ways. The Lord even encourages us to have His mind, to take on lifestyles of His ways, thoughts and in His likeness, for this is pleasing unto Him. Thereby, you can embrace that there is great joy in life in making simple the difficult and complex challenges of living. Do not get weary. Do not faint. Do not become overwhelmed when a giant appears as stress, or a storm comes your way as depression, or the threat of pestilence is possible as sickness. God is in control! *"I eagerly expect and hope that I will in no way be ashamed, but will have sufficient courage so that now as always Christ will be exalted in my body, whether by life or by death." (Philippians 1:20)* Through studying and gaining wisdom, the facts and truth will make you free to face giants and storms in the Lord's strength. The Lord fills and delivers those who seek and know Him with their hearts. They live in His principles, values and expectations of heaven and earth to dwell and exist within you to do His Will and freely take care of one another.

You must go through copulation to create the opportunity for life to be birthed through pains of childbearing labors and working with your hands as providers, which are the only ways to mature into manhood and womanhood. *"I the LORD search the heart and examine the mind, to reward each person according to their conduct, according to what their deeds deserve."* *(Jeremiah 17:10)* As with the difficulties that come with life, you must choose to forgive, restore and move forward. Simplicity of life is likened to eating wisely. Many people live to eat. However, this behavior is flawed, and people find themselves being gluttons without discipline and obedience. Choose to eat to live, not live to eat for this is good in the sight of the Lord. When you decide to love to live, you will begin to live to love, for the very person who is the love affair of your heart. When difficulties come your way, focus on the positive of the situation. Also, see yourself rising above the conditions and bringing resolutions to the challenge. Never focus on the negative energy of the person, for you will be drawn into the abyss of their hurt and pain, through your mind embracing negative energy. In doing so, the difficult becomes complex and loving to live dissipates.

At the end of the day, you are suffering in agony and perhaps defeat because you made the decision to not love to live. You should not allow your spirit, heart and character to take a bite of the P.I.E. of selfishness and pride. The Lord is on the side of those that keep the faith and love Him through the Son, in heaven and on earth spiritually. Stay the course, for life is the teacher of truth and the bearer of good and bad news. Good and bad remain constant throughout life and the earth. In your time of need, the Source has already predestined all creations that He will be available to His believers and favored people. In the Lord's spiritual engagement, you can breathe and speak with boldness and dominion authority to have the fulfillment of life in *the art of living.*

"Those the LORD has rescued will return. They will enter Zion with singing; everlasting joy will crown their heads. Gladness and joy will overtake them, and sorrow and sighing will flee away." (Isaiah 51:11)

ANTIDOTE 32 |
LIVE YOUR LIFE AWAKENED

"You must live life to the fullest to experience living abundantly."
Erogies Grigley, Jr.

Are your dreams interrupted with nightmares for a plan for a greater life? Dreams are the pathway to one's thoughts and sometimes what God desires for you. The nightmares can be that which you are confronted with in the deepest of trials or simply what you may have seen on television or witnessed in real life. Visions can usually be associated with where you are and what you desire in life, given by God and born out of your thoughts and actions. In all of this, visions and dreams can be inspired by the Lord for you to simply be in His Will and to do His Will without fear or compromise of the faith and work required. *"He had a dream in which he saw a stairway resting on the earth, with its top reaching to heaven, and the angels of God were ascending and descending on it." (Genesis 28:12)*

Wherever there is rise to your visions and dreams, there must be order in your mind, heart, spirit and will to commit and be focused on what is imagined, yet unseen. You must understand that the Creator and the Source did all things in creation by speaking power and authority through processes. Everything had a priority and order of sequence, as the Creator thought of the earth, universe, cosmos and all things and beings were manifested from the end to the beginning.

The Creator and the Source was committed to their vision and the outcome, all the way down to the smallest detail of an ant, leaf, raindrop and grain of sand. Everything has a purpose, for the Creator and the Source knows and understands that all things work together for the good and the purpose of the Sovereign's Will. No matter the task or project, the dream or the vision, you must have the courage and boldness to embark on the vision without allowing worldly talk, doubting thoughts and fear to enter into your domain and mind. There must be unequivocal belief, faith, courage and initiative to start the processes and complete the goal. Commence with speaking the final outcome to come forth, just as the Creator and the Source are one, fully on one accord, and inseparable in all, speaking with power and authority over all things. *"You must not listen to the words of that prophet or dreamer. The LORD your God is testing you to find out whether you love him with all your heart and with all your soul. It is the Lord your God you must follow, and him you must revere." (Deuteronomy 13:3)*

In your commitment to works and creation, you must do that which can be done in the light from early morning. The evening will come, and darkness will set in. Not only darkness, but also fatigue shall come upon you. You need to eat breakfast in the morning to be sustained through the day. You need to pray, study God's Word and open your heart for your spirit to be sustained in life. So, too, are the experiences, circle of loyal friends and details of the plan. You do not eat dinner for breakfast. It is out of order. Breakfast tastes better in the morning because the ingredients are designed for the morning appetite. Dinner settles the stomach for an evening rest. Likewise, spending time with the Lord allows you to fall asleep in good rest, for tomorrow's opportunities and commitment to the purpose of the dream and vision.

You must feed on the Word and nurture your faith in the trust, commitment and favor of the Lord. Therein, these tenants are results that are pleasing to yourself and the Source. There must be order to your vision and you must be committed to focus on Christ. The opportunities and challenges of integral successes lead to building upon the previous successes and challenges faced. Once you embrace this philosophy, you will soon experience the joy which will be great in your eyes and pleasing unto the Source. The vision will come to pass and be fulfilled by your hands while getting rest for tomorrow's promise. The purpose will come according to the deity and authority of the Source for the Creator's good pleasure and glory. That would-be wisdom is not the hindsight answer needed. Life requires foresight and insight with wisdom which must find her way into your vision and plan. Wisdom is critical, with knowledge and understanding, in order for the process to work. You embrace wisdom because you have chosen to be faithful before you ever started, with an attitude of seeing the task through. As you are faithful to the vision and the process through commitment to purpose, you can expect the vision will be fulfilled and goals accomplished for bearing good fruit.

Too often, life falls short and experiences unnecessary challenges and failures because there is no thinking through of what has been given to you. Wisdom is given to you to exercise in purpose and priorities, not pessimistic and little to no commitment. You cannot be lukewarm. Rather, be hot or cold, courageous and bold, faithful and truthful with aim. You cannot attempt to do that which must be done in the early morning for the late-night hour. These things require you to act in the moment, to seize the opportunity and bring closure. You cannot expect to have the same energy, power, opportunities and natural benefits that come with the light; nor, expect to feel and see the same as felt and seen in the moment of the vision, which is light and life of creation and success.

Wherever your heart is, so is your vision and treasurers! The greater the vision, the greater the test and challenge by the Source, as to the will of your heart to step into your promise and purpose. This endeavor leads to the many destinations of successes and accomplishments, favored by the

Source and the Creator, towards your ultimate destiny and the Creator's glory. You who maturely believe and have a strong constitution of great faith and great works of substance and excellence possess the necessary spiritual power and inner strength. These are given by the Source to avail as your greatest friend, for the purpose and promise at hand. The promise and purpose must come to pass and be fulfilled in due season by the one chosen, as the Source and the Creator cannot lie. *"For where your treasure is, there your heart will be also." (Matthew 6:21)*

Failure to embrace the Source as your inner strength and peace towards excellence is from your selfishness, ego and pride. Failure to resist naysayers and the unfamiliar voice of the enemy shall deceive you to reach outward to discover your greatest worse enemy who shares the same residence in the world. The residence of these three foes – selfishness, pride and ego – weigh three pounds and is six inches in diameter, and two hemispheres separate them with untapped capacity. It is estimated that you who are superior generates greater brain use, and an average person less brain use, based on what a person believes and does to exercise the brain. The enlightenment to exceed cognitive and exercise spiritual powers is foreign to most. Foreign because of rational and logical reasoning of your brain that produces unbelief, making the Source's spiritual access often rarely attempted or understood. Faith and submission to purpose are perspectives linked by the Source to produce a victorious life. Spiritual awakening is linked to help you make it to each destination of successes that ultimately lead you into the perfect destiny: Peace, Joy and Favor, with Christ.

The challenge for many is that they lack great faith and live lukewarm lives in perspective and attitude, chasing after meaningless toils. They do not chase after the truths, which establishes Jesus Christ as Lord, Master and Redeemer for thousands of years, un-phased and fully alive today. The Lord desires to be your greatest asset, greatest friend and greatest weapon against that which prevails against the purpose and destiny He has placed in you.

Again, all things, not some things, when the Kingdom of Heaven is greater than self and the cause, will always work together for those that love the Lord and remain committed to the tests and the processes. The Lord says that one-day with Him is like a thousand of earth years, which you should be aware of such a phenomenon. *"A thousand years in your sight are like a day that has just gone by, or like a watch in the night." (Psalm 90:4)* You must measure the success of your day daily by doing something greater than for self. Putting this in perspective, when we spend a full day with God, know that billions are trying to reach Him at the same time, for motives only known to them and the Source. But God can handle all the prayers and calls for Him to help those in need. So, in half of a day in the Lord's time, 500 years of accomplishments, experiences and circumstances of changes and evolutions take place which you cannot comprehend. What have you accomplished in a half day's work? In the infantry, we would say, "We get more done before nine o'clock a.m. than most people get done all day!"

You must understand that time and timing, patience and control are everything to both purpose, destinations, successes, opportunities and your ultimate destiny. Most times, it is far better for you to understand that the Source's testing and sometimes the breaking must occur before the first and next great thing you desire. Whatever you want to have and desire to achieve will be presented before you by the Source, which are in His Will. Learn to let the Source meet you as you are and where you are, for in this moment, you will be changed, transformed and transcend the small minded and inferior person that you truly were without the Source in your life. If you choose to do a thing, you must not only have a vision, but preparations must be made with every level of detail from the largest pieces to the tiniest of them, both in material things, and mental and spiritual things that cannot be seen by the physical eyes; but crystal clear in spiritual vision and sight. *"So when you are assembled and I am with you in spirit, and the power of our Lord Jesus is present, hand this man over to Satan for the destruction of the flesh, so that his spirit may be saved on the day of the Lord." (1 Corinthians 5:4-5)*

The beginning of your purpose is in your voice speaking the vision into existence, through the Lord and His spirit, in order for you to believe and commit. Take baby steps towards building your faith to soar with wings of eagles and wave your fingers through the clouds, enroute to the stars of your life. You must be tested before the Source will give you increase. Increase requires responsibility and accountability proven from being over a little or faithful over a lot. Increase only comes by knowledge, wisdom, understanding and performing your best regardless of the conditions, to prepare you for the opportunity when it comes. In other words, your perception of half empty or half full will determine if it is impossible or possible.

Positive personal attitude and trust, with an abiding faith is everything to purpose and opportunity. This is where courage and strength come from in the given power of the Source that is with you. This is why you must start early, eat breakfast (knowledge and wisdom foods) and give your all to whatever comes your way with great faith and excellence to fulfill the vision to the highest. Often times, fulfilling is to defeat the very thing or person that stands between you and the opportunity that will propel you into your purpose for the next great opportunity. Never settle for embracing mediocrity, everything has value to where you were, but also to where you are and are purposed to go.

The Source and the Creator speaks this embracement and commandment by authority, *"And we know that in all things God works together for the good of those that love him, who are called according to his purpose." (Roman 8:28)* When you face your problem as part of your purpose with unmovable courage and unshakable faith, you will take a giant step into your future and favored opportunities. Opportunities that will multiply, upon multiplying, as the Source will give the increase to the purpose as long as you are willing and ask the right questions. Out of your dreams come your vision and your future. If you believe and have great faith, you will perform great woks and do exceedingly well in what you love.

See that the vision is yours. The vision is simply the Source's purpose, good or bad, to be tested in your faith and belief. Tested and blessed takes place in order for you to find favor in the Lord through your excellence of works for the Source. At all times, in the light and in darkness, in pain and joy, abasing and abounding, the Source desires the best for you. It is never about you. It is all about whether the Source and Creator can trust you out of the tests that were presented before you, to glorify the Father. *"And afterward, I will pour out my Spirit on all people. Your sons and daughters will prophesy, your old men will dream dreams, your young men will see visions." (Joel 2:28)*

Many times, the Source will not allow you to enter your purpose, except that you go through your enemy. An enemy combined of logic of the mind, education, credentials and environmental posse that promotes self. This enemy is not a cause greater than self, and it does not embrace faith of the spirit in the Spirit for a great cause to the higher deity of life. Defeating the setback in the battle space of your mind can move you forward with purpose, clothed in the full armor of God. If you believe in your heart, the favor and faithfulness of the Source will be realized.

Let not mental gymnastics hide the spiritual door of opportunities that you must go through for enlightenment and the new dimension of your purpose. Your vision and purpose are about a relationship which includes suffering and abundance, which is the process that you should not focus on. Your focus in your faith and testing must be on what is in front of you, not what you are going through. Although Jesus despised going to the cross initially, He found strength in God the Creator and Father to embrace the cross and its suffering and shame. He was able to do so because of His insight and foresight was on the joy before Him. He trusted the process of the faith that He knew was in reach by His Father's Word. In three days, God said that He shall raise Jesus's temple, to return to the Father and sit again in His deity, having defeated death and the enemy. Forget about your past and those things behind you. You have to take on a new attitude and accept to be pruned. Even when you are bearing fruit, you must stand firm. Pruning is good, for what you are focused on is the new wine, which shall be poured into the new wine skin. The old you must die in order for the true you to rise and live fully. Your journey begins in the testing and the struggle coming to conclusion, for which you will never go back through the path or lifestyle you are victorious over, again.

Once you defeat the enemy in your mind, you can run with the Spirit of the Lord to defeat everything counter and that which held you back from moving into your promise. Along the path and journey of life's different destinations, the promise of Christ is key to your destiny, for Christ is not a liar. Not only shall you bring forth good fruit, you will have a strong hedge of protection around you and blessings upon you. You are a continuous blessing for buds, blossoms and bearing good fruit in the right season which is always right on time. Stay connected to the Source and move with wisdom, courage and patience. The Source is focused on bringing the given vision to a heightened reality of change, perfection and stability to scale in trust and faith, in relationship and favor with the Source, the Vine. Your charge is to hear the Word, listen to the instructions and understand the secrets revealed to why you went through the tests. Your charge is to begin running and not get weary or faint, not overcome with fear. Focus on being on a strong foundation. Mount up with great courage to take flight like an eagle, and embrace the courage of a prizefighter, jabbing and punching your way into your future. With the favor, help and blessing of the Source, you shall arrive at your vision's manifestation of *the art of living* and your final destiny, paradise and life eternal with Jesus Christ.

"These are the visions I saw while lying in bed: I looked,
and there before me stood a tree in the middle of the land. Its height was enor-
mous. The tree grew large and strong and its top touched the sky;
it was visible to the ends of the earth." (Daniel 4:10-11)

ANTIDOTE 33 |
CAPTURE THE MOMENTS
AND MEMORIES

"One's success is found in their love for doing the same thing every day in excellence, which kindles passion and joy." Erogies Grigley Jr.

When your days are filled with fault finding, downfalls and overwhelming pressures, how do you shift towards a greater and more positive energy? In life, we must let go of the phantoms of what we do not have and live life surrounding not only what we have, but in the power of what is possible in the excellence of Christ. *"Those who think they know something do not yet know as they ought to know." (1 Corinthians 8:2)*

Our minds are battlefields for life and death, in spirit and in truth, waged with a torrent of attacks to torment and defenses for good and peace. The days and nights sometime run parallel, as we find ourselves in the midst of pressures from self and others. There are remedies to this way of thinking to achieve quality of life, requiring a renewing of the mind and spirit, being filled in your heart, through the Holy Spirit. As a person thinks, so are they in their heart.

Awesome art, writing, cooking, songs and poems are motions in the moment of life which create smiles and sometimes tears. The emotions are manifested from what is seen in the heart to be made perfect for the giver and receiver. All things that are negative should not be credited to evil. Many times, it is either what you have done or what God did or did not allow in order to fix you for His glory. Bringing you in line during such a perfect moment of healing and relationship with Him is paramount to trust and faith for His faithfulness. *"Frustration is better than laughter, because a sad face is good for the heart. The heart of the wise is in the house of mourning, but the heart of fools is in the house of pleasure." (Ecclesiastes 7:3-4)*

To some, faults and downfalls are triggered by evil. I believe evil has nothing to do with most events and receives too much credit. Many times, a person's actions are a result of ignorance, selfish motives, ego, pride, lack of control, disobedience and poo judgment. You must not stoop to the judgment of others to cover them in unfair false perceptions. Stop seeking them out. Rather, let yourself know that the latter is not the aim of the discovery of greatness. It is the resilient pursuit of what you believe and the greatness residing in you for fulfillment, planted by the Father. You must love doing the same thing every day for the passion to be kindled and your purpose to burn brilliantly!

When the flames no longer burn with a glow and generate warmth, the joy and love will dissipate. All who see you will know that your spirit has been struck to become out of alignment for your gifting to be perfected. Your gift is not your own. Your gift is the Lord's to be used for sharing with the people and glorifying Him in honor and praise. It is entirely too tempting to take on the role of a little god and begin to judge people, things, statements and relationships. Under the Constitution, free speech allows you to express your views and subconsciously to pursue liberties, regardless of the pain you may cause others. But, with Christ, you are to refrain from foolish talk and selfish positions, for these slashes into the fabrics that forge love, humility and servitude.

To counter this behavior requires spiritual and noble character intervention, to guide your thinking. Take your spouse, children and your health. Regardless of the time or place, the mounting attacks on your principles and body, you can care for those close to you and be there for them. You cannot change or heal anyone in your own power, but you can contribute to their change and healing. Four things no one has been able to stop for thousands of years – not to get ill, not to pay taxes, not to age and not to die. *"Above all else, guard your heart, for everything you do flows from it."* (Proverbs 4:23)

Guard your heart and your gifts while using your gifting to help and bless others. Use your gifts unto the Lord, to gift something of meaning and beauty to someone who has much less. If you work out your indifferences and conclude on one accord on the matter, the circumstances will change, and the indifferences resolved. Make room in your tabernacle for healthy and respectable debate to matters of the mind in spirit and heart. As you speak to the Source and the Creator for increase, just be still, while being about good works. Watch, wait and pray in your watchtower for God to move. He sees you are focused on the outcome for the future existence, not last year or yesterday. Therefore, each person saved, just and righteous and who believes have already been given success so that God can have the victory in Jesus Christ, in using them for his purpose and glory.

Imagine the smiles from the acts of kindness and gestures of love. Make the gift and create the smiles from the acts of kindness and gestures of love through art, writing, cooking, poems and songs! Now, aren't you smiling? Aren't you filled with joy and a great sense of purpose and contribution? As art, writing, cooking and singing promote unity within self and the corporate body of the family and church, you must embrace creating positive energy. You must yoke up and come together to reason as brothers and sisters, virtues and morals united in family and friends to achieve greatness. *"And this is my prayer: that your love may abound more and more in knowledge and depth of insight, so that you may be able to discern what is best and may be pure and blameless for the day of Christ, filled with the fruit of righteousness that comes through Jesus Christ--to the glory and praise of*

God." *(Philippians 1:9-11)* When in plain sight, there is nothing to be had, but in spirit and demonstration unto God, love will cover a multitude of problems and misunderstandings.

My grandmother had a saying, "Be home before 12:00 am for there is nothing good that is going to happen that time of night, except it is Satan's busiest time". You have the ability to let life be free of drama and let love treat everyone equally at every establishment of the heart that is visited. You have to change mediocrity, lethargic, mendacious and self-righteous behaviors to change your lifestyle. This mediocrity and less than desired follies above have gone on way to long. You must realize and know God is on the side of the righteous and just, with an open court to hear what man has to say. The Word of God remarks, *"I was young and now I am old, yet I have never seen the righteous forsaken or their children begging for bread."* (Psalm 37:25) You have to declare life as you have observed and lived for yourself, family and friends; and, the sick and the poor. The matters of generosity, modesty and speaking wonderful things in optimism and freedoms to self and others, will increase your joy, peace and favor. So, if you enjoy the apron and love to bake and cook, draw and paint art, write poems and sing songs, only to trade them in for foolishness, *the art of living* is not for you.

*"Now, brothers and sisters, about times and dates we do not need
to write to you, for you know very well that the day of the Lord will come like
a thief in the night." (1 Thessalonians 5:1-2)*

BY WHOSE
AUTHORITY?

The Holy Spirit is adjoined to the Source, and thereby, must glorify God in all things and ways, regardless of your desires, faithfulness or righteousness. We will receive with authority the Word of the Lord and impart knowledge, wisdom and understanding unto the one who is humble and faithful in righteousness with patience and a zeal to learn.

The Source reminds all, not just the chosen ones, that the Father, God Himself has given Jesus Christ everything, all power, dominion, authority and reign on earth and in heaven, forging the glorious living in the Holy Spirit. Wisdom and blessings come from the Lord, and He gives what He desires by authority, as a declaration to the one who will hear and listen to the Word of the Source. *"Forging the glorious in the Holy Spirit to thus from the Lord and give what is His by authority, as a declaration to the one who will hear and listen to the words of the Source. In reading this, then, you will be able to understand my insight into the mystery of Christ, which was not made known to people in other generations as it has now been revealed by the Spirit to God's holy apostles and prophets." (Ephesians 3:4-5)*

The 'path' is receiving God's divine Word and accepting His Son Jesus Christ's unconditional love, and to serve as His earthly spiritual agent. Your 'journey' is physical and spiritual in obedient and righteous living as a servant and disciple. Your 'purpose' is made sufficient to embrace an absolute clear direction for your contentment is solely God's divine

Will for your life. His perfection and Sovereignty will lead you to your 'destiny' which is returning to stand and kneel before the King of Kings, Jesus Christ on behalf of God the Father. In this place, on holy ground, Jesus will establish your final destiny for your spirit and soul. There you will be safe in the midst of the great gulf that divides Paradise and Hades, as you take a walk to one of the two gates guarded by Great Angels and Cheribums.

May you come into the fullness of a relationship with Jesus Christ where you can find to whom you belong, as His own. Jesus Christ will change your life for the better and together with Him, you will make it through all things and have all that you will ever need. Never forsaken, never separated, never unloved, never without. He will always leave you with purpose and clarity to your path for *the art of living well.* May the peace and joy of the Lord be upon you and His rich love and abundance of favor consume you like fire as He smears you with His grace!

Today, your ways of old have been enlightenment for you to transcend into the better and greater you. Enjoy your journey. Stay on the path of simplicity and righteousness, and discover your purpose in *the art of living well!*

PRAYER

Lord God, Heavenly Father,

You are adored in all of your majesty. You are given thanks in gratefulness for your faithfulness and unconditional love. Thank you for the wisdom of your Word to be a lamp unto all eyes, and light unto all feet, minds and hearts who lift these words unto their bosom, spirit and soul. I pray for a spiritual and new mindset enlightenment upon the readers who choose The Art of Living Well as a way of life. Lord, the way of life and our attitude is in Jesus Christ, our glorious Lord, and His abundant grace and mercy. Thank you for life, love and living in your pavilion where there are green pastures, covered with lilies and lilacs, besides peaceful waters.

"For this reason, I kneel before the Father, from whom every family in heaven and on earth derives its name. I pray that out of his glorious riches he may strengthen you with power through his Spirit in your inner being, so that Christ may dwell in your hearts through faith. And I pray that you, being rooted and established in love, may have power, together with all the Lord's holy people, to grasp how wide and long and high and deep is the love of Christ, and to know this love that surpasses knowledge—that you may be filled to the measure of all the fullness of God." (Ephesians 3:14-19)

Forever Your friend, Rev. Roe

TRANSCEND YOUR OLD WAYS INTO ENLIGHTENMENT

Your Purpose. Your Journey. Your Destiny.

Because Jesus Christ loves you and loved you first, the Father also loves you unconditionally. They are inseparable, as is the relationship they desire to have with you, which you can have through your free will spiritual choice. Trust in the Lord. Let Him prove Himself mighty in your life. Test the Lord, and He will answer your clean heart, sound mind, loving spirit and holy tabernacle for His Spirit's indwelling. Because of a more excellent covenant and better promises in Christ, He replaced the first covenant which was obsolete. Which was not faultless and made right with the second covenant through his divine shed blood, sacrifice of His life as a ransom and through His resurrection. You no longer have to be afar off from an intimate relationship with Jesus, as He is risen and is always near.

Today, you have total and full personal access through the Holy Spirit which is how God communicates with you and endures a permanent relationship with you in a covenant that is binding in agreement and cannot be broken. Consider connecting to the Source, where you can draw strength, find peace and joy, and have all of your needs supplied. Try Jesus! You will not regret your decision today by inviting Jesus Christ into your heart, making Him your Lord and Savior. This I promise, along with your name will be written in the Lamb's Book of Life to have life abundantly in this life and life everlasting with Him in Heaven. (Hebrews 8:6-12)

ABOUT EROGIES 'ROE' GRIGLEY JR.

Reverend, Lieutenant Colonel (Retired) Erogies 'Roe' Grigley Jr. is the Co-Pastor of The Alabaster House Ministry, retired federal Division Director, and a retired U.S. Army officer. He was born in Sanford, Florida in 1957 to Jannie Mae Kimble Grigley and Erogies Grigley Sr.

Roe began his military career in the U.S. Army in 1975 as an infantryman. He joined the Army Reserves in Orlando, FL in 1980. He graduated from Seminole High School and is a 1984 Distinguished Military Student and Distinguished Military Graduate of the University of Central Florida's College of Army ROTC and from the Army's Command and General Staff College in 1997. He also completed numerous graduate level courses, business and executive seminars, and read over 500 books on relationships, ministry, business, leadership, management and philosophy. He played college football for the University of Central Florida and semi-professional football for the Fort Benning Doughboys of Fort Benning, Georgia.

Roe is married to the former Valerie Denise Saunders. They have three children: Ebony, Erogies III, and Erin; and five grandchildren: Amir, Aniah, Austin, Alex and Ashton.

Lieutenant Colonel Grigley's career includes serving as Division Director, Federal Protective Service. His previous 30-years of military assignments include: Human Resources Director – Equal Opportunity/

Sexual Assault Programs, Third US Army/Combined Forces Land Component Command, Ft McPherson, Georgia (Africa & Middle East); Commander (Interim), Chief of Staff/Executive Officer, Army & Air Force Exchange Service – Pacific Region, Okinawa, Japan, employing over 8,100 employees and operates over 1,400 retail stores and restaurant operations covering Alaska, Guam, Hawaii, Japan, Korea, Okinawa and Thailand; Deputy Director, DoD Policy for Aerial Delivery, Field Services and Training Directorate, Ft Lee, VA; Chief Instructor, Pre-Command Course and Airborne Orientation Course, Ft Lee, VA; Chief, Kosovo Logistics Plans & Multi-National Agreements (U.S., United Arab Emirates, Kosovo, Allied Forces), Stuttgart, Germany; Senior Logistics Advisor, Czech Republic and Slovenia Ministries of Defense (in-country); Executive Officer, 266th Quartermaster Battalion, Ft Lee, VA; Director of Security, Operations, Training and Education/S-3, 17th Area Support Group, Camp Zama, Japan; Deputy Director, Installation and Regional Support Operations, United States Army, Camp Zama, Japan; HHC Company Commander, 35th Supply & Services Battalion, Sagami Depot, Japan; Commander, Alpha Company, 197th Support Battalion, 197th Infantry Brigade, Ft Benning, GA; Director, Support Operations & Commander, Charlie Company, 324th Support Battalion, 24th Infantry Division, Saudi Arabia (Iraq); Battalion S-2/3, 197th Support Battalion, 197th Infantry Brigade, Ft Benning, GA; Chief, Logistics Branch, 1st Corps Support Command, Ft Bragg, NC; Battalion S-4, 18th Personnel & Administration Battalion, Ft Bragg, NC; Platoon Leader and Company Executive Officer, 612th Quartermaster Company, Ft Bragg, NC; Personnel and Training Officer, 442 Personnel Service Battalion, Army Reserves, Orlando, FL; Team Leader, 1st Battalion, 58th Infantry, Ft Benning, GA; Team Leader, 1st Battalion, 9th Infantry, 2nd Infantry Division, Camp Hovey, Korea

Lieutenant Colonel Grigley's education highlights include: Diploma, Army Command and General Staff College (12-month graduate resident program); Bachelor of Arts, University of Central Florida; Army Logistics Management Officer's Advance Course (5-month resident); Sexual Assault and Victim Advocate Intervention and Resolution Course; Leadership Awareness - Equal Opportunity Course (Defense Equal Opportunity Management Institute); Army Human Resource Management Course, Alexandria, VA; Director of Logistics Management Course (graduate level); Dispute Resolution and Mediation Course, The Justice Center of Atlanta; Total Quality Management and Process Improvements, Camp Zama, Japan; Air Force Contract Management Course Certification, resident program; Combined Arms Staff Course (3-month graduate resident); Contracting To The Federal Government Certification, Fayetteville Technical Institute; Small Business Management Program, Fayetteville Technical Institute; Air Logistics Delivery and Maintenance Course; Strategic Mobility Planners Course; Army Logistics Management Officer's Basic Course (5 month resident); Advance Infantry Training Course

Lieutenant Colonel Grigley's awards and recognition include: Legion of Merit; Bronze Star; Distinguished Order of Saint Martin Medal; Meritorious Service Medal (3); Joint Service Commendation Medal; Army Commendation Medal (2); Army Achievement Medal (4); Navy - Marine Corps Achievement Medal; Military Outstanding Volunteer Service Medal; Korea Service Medal; Kuwait Liberation Medal – Kuwait; Kuwait Liberation Medal - Saudi Arabia; Good Conduct Medal; National Defense Service Medal (2); Global War on Terrorism Medal; Armed Forces Reserve Medal; Overseas Service Medal (3); Senior Parachutist Badge; Parachute Rigger Badge